Planning IT

Planning IT

Creating an information management strategy

David J. Silk

BUTTERWORTH
HEINEMANN

Butterworth–Heinemann Ltd
Linacre House, Jordan Hill, Oxford OX2 8DP

🌐 PART OF REED INTERNATIONAL BOOKS

OXFORD LONDON BOSTON
MUNICH NEW DELHI SINGAPORE SYDNEY
TOKYO TORONTO WELLINGTON

First published 1991
Paperback edition 1992

British Library Cataloguing in Publication Data
Silk, David J.
   Planning IT: Creating an information management
   strategy.
   I. Title
   658.400285

ISBN 0 7506 0832 3

Typeset by Vision Typesetting, Manchester
Printed and bound in Great Britain by
Redwood Press Ltd, Melksham, Wiltshire

Contents

Preface

'Information' is a difficult concept. It is closely bound up with everything we do, yet it is intangible and of little value on its own. For managers, the value of information lies in the extent to which it contributes to good decision-making and effective action.

Practising managers hear much about the value of information, and of Information Technology and Systems (IT/IS). Phrases like 'information as the enabler of organizational change' and 'sustainable competitive advantage from IT' press for attention and some positive response. Yet managers must be hard-nosed about these issues; investment in this aspect of the business must be weighed against the many other demands for limited resources.

This book is designed for senior practising managers who wish to improve the use of information for the corporate benefit of their enterprises. It takes the 'general management' perspective – concerned with the organization as a whole rather that just one functional part of it. It does not include a lot of factual information about IT/IS. Such information is widely available elsewhere, and in any case should not be the immediate concern of the senior manager. It offers practical guidance in a form which is intelligible to general managers. It gives practical examples but avoids being dogmatic or prescriptive in detail. Rather, it is designed to help you as a manager think the issues through for yourself, so that *you* can be prescriptive about *your* organization.

This approach should be of value to managers, from a wide range of disciplines (including IT/IS), who wish to take the holistic, general management view of their enterprise. The book will provide such managers with a framework for assessing and improving the practice of information management in their organizations.

After an introductory chapter the book develops six related guidelines for information management. You are strongly recommended to study the book in the sequence of the chapters. This will provide the clearest picture, and lead to the most effective action plan for you and your organization.

I hope that you enjoy using the book, and that it contributes to improved business performance in your enterprise.

David J. Silk

1 Introduction

The aim of this book

The aim of this book is to provide senior managers with a framework for assessing and improving the practice of information management in their organizations. The preface explained this aim more fully. The book is practical, and intended for non-specialists. It helps *you* diagnose the situation in *your* enterprise, and generate an appropriate action plan. It thereby helps you, as a general manager, to make a more proactive and informed response to the opportunities of modern Information Technology and Systems (IT/IS). This is what good information management is all about.

The book is not a primer about IT/IS. The technology is advancing rapidly, and the systems evolve at different rates in different places and countries. If you feel the need for some factual information about IT/IS, you may find the following books useful. Full details of books referred to are given in References at the end of each chapter.

- Zorkoczy (1990). This gives a good overview, both of the technology and of current systems. Part 1 of the book takes a broad view of the impact of IT on work and society. It gives a wide range of examples, including the use of information by managers and office workers.
- Eaton, Smithers and Curran (1988). This is a readable but more detailed book about IT. It also sets IT into a managment and social context. It will be useful for those with a line responsibility for the IS function, or with a closer interest in the technical background.
- Knight and Silk (1990). This book covers both IT/IS and information management (IM) at an introductory general management level. As you might expect, its approach is broadly consistent with the approach of this book.

The approach

When you have finished studying this book, I don't want you to think 'Yes, but what do I do next?' Most managers are in that position already: they recognize the significance of information management, but they don't quite know how to set about getting it right in their organization. Instead, the book will help you develop an action plan whose items you fully understand and which you believe you will be able to implement. In that way I hope you will be able to say 'Right. That's helped me to think this issue through; now I can get on with it'.

This book therefore requires an active partnership between me, the writer, and you, the reader. Like all partnerships, we are both going to have to work hard at it. Here's how:

- For my part, I shall try to make the book concise, relevant, and readable. I shall illustrate the ideas from my experience of dealing with senior managers and organizations who have faced a wide range of problems in the area of information management.
- For your part, you will need to give the book your serious attention, and work right through it. You will need to think about the questions posed, and consider the answers which apply to your enterprise. You will need to assemble this into an action plan, in the way indicated in the book.

If we work together in this way, there should be some real benefit!

The structure

The book is based on six guidelines for information management. These guidelines were developed in a business school and a practical environment, in two ways:

- By taking account of the results of recent surveys of general managers, asking which issues of information management give them the greatest concern. The results of these surveys have been published elsewhere (Silk, 1989 and 1990).
- By discussing with individual managers, and groups of managers, the most effective approaches to take in dealing with these major issues of information management.

The structure of the book is shown in Figure 1.1.

This first chapter introduces and explains the six guidelines. Chapters 2–7 then address each of them in more detail. Each of those chapters ends with a set of questions which you should consider in the context of yourself and your

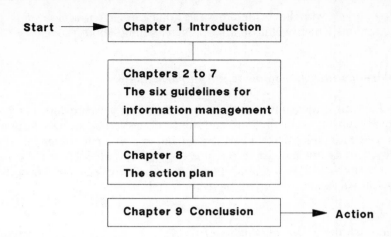

Figure 1.1   *Structure of the book*

enterprise. This will produce a score, and some action points, as part of an information management audit. They will be carried forward to help you construct your action plan.

Chapter 8 draws both the book and your audit together. You will produce a consolidated action plan which is structured according to the timescale of the individual actions (short- or long-term) and according to whether they are personal or team actions in your enterprise. The detail and relevance of this action plan will be the tangible evidence of your study of the book. The subsequent success in implementing the action plan will be the tangible evidence of your competence as a manager!

Chapter 9 provides a short conclusion to the book, consolidates its main points, and exhorts you to action.

The six guidelines

The six guidelines for information management which we shall be developing are as follows:

1   Establish an information management partnership.
2   Distinguish the potential benefits of IT/IS.
3   Think strategically about information management.
4   Identify the benefits, and their value.
5   Manage the achievement of the benefits.
6   Prepare for the future.

Let's see briefly what lies behind these six guidelines, in terms of the ideas and the questions which will arise in a manager's mind about them.

Establish an information management partnership

This is about establishing an effective partnership between top managers, middle managers/users of IT/IS, and the IT professionals. Good information management requires such a partnership, but in practice it is often either not achieved or is imbalanced. What are the appropriate roles for the three players? How can senior managers cultivate the right level of co-operation? How will you know when you have got it right?

Distinguish the potential benefits of IT/IS

The so-called generic benefits of IT/IS are efficiency, effectiveness, and strategic advantage (or competitive edge). The organization must distinguish between these generic benefits, and then actively seek each type of benefit which is relevant to its business situation. This is necessary because the management context and perception of an information system are as important as the system itself. How does the manager strike the right balance between the three generic benefits? Should the organization be out there in front, or following behind, in its use of IT/IS?

Think strategically about information management

For many organizations information management is now important enough to support, or even drive, strategic change in the business. Senior managers now need to adopt a systematic approach to business strategy, including the 'information' aspect alongside others. This will require a range of conceptual frameworks for the manager to try out with himself and his colleagues. How can the manager deal with the fact that the business situation does not stand still – that competitive advantage is never long-lasting? What are the principles for achieving sustainable competitive advantage?

Identify the benefits, and their value

This is more specific than Guideline 2, which dealt with generic benefits. Here you need to be very specific about what benefits you plan to achieve from your investment in IT/IS, how you can quantify them, and how you can determine whether they have in fact been achieved. The business case for investment in IT/IS needs to be better than an act of faith, and must be related to the general investment culture of the organization. But how is it possible to deal with both the 'hard' and the 'soft' benefits of IT/IS? Is the senior manager necessarily at loggerheads with the IT professionals and the accountants over this?

Manage the achievement of the benefits

Having decided on the generic and specific benefits, management needs to take positive action to make sure the benefits really happen. There needs to be a champion of change at senior level, and delegated responsibilities at lower levels. You need to allocate clear responsibilities, but how can you integrate this with the other aspects of planning an information system? Does post-implementation audit become a witch-hunt when things go wrong? If so, is there a better way of doing things?

Prepare for the future

IT/IS and the business situation are changing rapidly. 'Change' is the keynote of the 1990s. Managers should therefore keep under periodic review the relevant technical advances (which are potential opportunities), the changing nature of the business, and the link between the organization's corporate strategy and its information strategy. The experts are predicting the 'information-based organization' as the model for the 1990s. Is your management facilitating the change to this style of operation? Is this the exclusive problem of senior management, or is it something that should be handled more pervasively in the organization?

At this level of detail these guidelines all sound rather like motherhood statements: convincing enough for us to nod assent to, but not specific enough to help with our practical problems as managers. It is the aim of the next six chapters to explain and illustrate the principles more fully, and invite you to consider them in your particular context. This should make them come alive and relevant.

The information management audit

Your consideration of the guidelines should lead progressively to a practical action plan. To help you with this, at the end of each of the next six chapters I will invite you to take stock of the situation in your current organization. This forms one part of your information management audit. Thus there are six parts altogether.

The format for each part of the audit is given in Figure 1.2.

Guideline			
Ser.	**Question**	**Score**	**Action**
1			
2			
3			
4			
5			
6			
7			
8			
9			
10			
	TOTALS		

Figure 1.2   *IM audit – format*

For each guideline you will be asked to consider ten questions about the current situation for yourself and your organization. You should put an honest score against each question. Use a subjective scale, with 10 being the best possible score, and 0 the worst possible score. I call it a subjective scale because I am inviting you to be ruthlessly self-critical. Thus you should try to ensure that there is a fair spread of scores, with an average of about 5. Remember, we can all do better, and we might all be worse! You should indicate in the 'Action' column all those questions for which you scored yourself below 5.

Finally, complete the two 'Total' boxes at the bottom of the form: the total score (which therefore becomes a percentage score for this guideline) and the total number of questions for which you score below 5. If your score is above 75 per cent ask yourself if you are really being honest; if your score is below 25 per cent ask yourself if things are really that bad.

The questions relating to each of the six IM audit forms are introduced and explained in the corresponding chapters. There are also copies of the forms, together, in Appendix 1, so that you can use them conveniently as a working document. If you make working copies of the forms, remember that they are protected by copyright. Please do not look ahead at the forms until you have studied the relevant chapter.

The action plan

In Chapter 8 you will bring together the six parts of your IM audit. You will of course focus on those things which need improving. For each of these you will identify the 'impelling' and 'impeding' factors for reaching a practical solution. Finally, you will decide what needs to be done by you and by others, both in the short and the long term.

This progressive building up of the action plan should mean that you 'own it', that you believe in it, and that you think you can realistically make progress with it. This should give the highest possible assurance that you will succeed in practice. Let's now work together to achieve that.

References

Eaton, J., Smithers, J. and Curran, S. (1988), *This is IT – A Manager's Guide to Information Technology*, 2nd Ed, Philip Allan. ISBN 0-86003-660-X (paperback).

Knight, A. V. and Silk, D. J. (1990), *Managing Information*, McGraw-Hill. ISBN 0-07-707086-0 (hardback).

Silk, D. J. (1989), 'Current Issues in Information Management', *Int. J. of Info. Mgt*, Vol. 9, No. 2 (June), pp. 85–9.

Silk, D. J. (1990), 'Current Issues in Information Management – Update', *Int. J. of Info. Mgt*, Vol. 10, no 3 (Sep.), pp. 178–81.

Zorkoczy, P. (1990), *Information Technology – An Introduction*, 3rd Ed, Pitman. ISBN 0-273-03238-0 (paperback).

2 The information management partnership

Introduction

The first of our six guidelines is 'Establish an information management partnership'. In a sense this is the foundation: it provides the management framework within which you can apply all the other principles. Failure here is going to make it very difficult to achieve effective information systems. Success here can at least ensure that information systems are considered carefully, decisions are made consciously rather than by default, and the decisions made are given whole-hearted support.

The key players in the information management (IM) partnership are:

- Top managers.
- Middle managers, and other users of IT/IS.
- IT professionals.

Together they form what has sometimes been called the triangle of conflict, or the ITernal triangle. In Figure 2.1 it is called the IM triangle, and will be used as an agenda or model for the discussion in the rest of this chapter.

First, we'll consider the characteristics and appropriate role for each of these key players, and the changes in behaviour which you, as a senior manager, would like to encourage. Then we shall consider the organizational measures which you might take to help them develop, and work more effectively together. Finally, you should take stock of the situation in your own enterprise, and note the relevant points for your action plan. Figure 2.5 will help you with this.

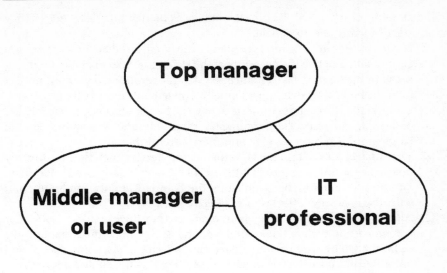

Figure 2.1 *The IM triangle*

The top manager

Top managers are responsible for the direction and control of the whole organization, or of a significant part of it. They formulate strategy and policy for the business, and direct its implementation. Their planning usually has a time-horizon of years, except when (as quite often happens) they are engaged in shorter-term reactions or 'firefighting'.

Senior managers are distinguished by the nature of the management thinking they perform, and the time-horizon of planning for which they take responsibility. Age doesn't matter; it's the type of work and the level of responsibility and influence which single out the top manager.

Although top managers, by definition, are competent and successful people, they are often the major problem in the IM triangle. There are several possible reasons for this:

(a) They may have had little to do with IT/IS during their careers. There was probably not much of it about when they were at the earlier stages, progressing first as functional managers and then as general managers. Like most of us, they do not like admitting their ignorance by dabbling in things they don't understand.

(b) They may be reluctant to try to learn more about IT/IS and its use. They don't want to show their lack of manual skill and confidence in front of their PA (who is far faster on the machinery than they could, or ever should, be). They fear the time it will take from their busy schedules if they start to learn and to dabble.

(c) However, they are assiduous readers of the quality and business press, and cannot fail to notice the accounts of the strategic impact of IT/IS on many areas of business today. Finance, banking, operations planning, project management, marketing, personnel management, inter-company transactions, and the customer interface have all been radically changed by the creative use of IT/IS. They are uneasy about this, and suspect they should be giving the subject greater and more careful thought.

(d) They may be locked into the view that 'computers' (which they mistakenly take to be the entire scope of IT/IS) are all to do with operational efficiency, and should therefore be handled by the IT professionals, in conjunction with the operational levels of management.

(e) Alternatively they may seize upon some idea they have seen in the press, or a demonstration they have attended, and decide that this is going to be right for their organization. This can be called showing vision and initiative, but if the idea is ill-conceived, then it can be a disaster both for the organization and for lower levels of management.

You may recognize some of these symptoms in the top managers in your organization. You may even be one yourself, and the cap fits uncomfortably well. In either case, let's consider the type of behaviour which we need to cultivate and encourage in top managers. The key points might be as follows.

As a top manager, you should take an intelligent interest in what the journals and the quality press tell us about:

1   Advances in IT/IS. New technology and systems can offer important opportunities for businesses.
2   Applications of IT/IS in the same or similar sectors of industry. In this fast-moving field companies cannot afford to drop behind the industry norm, and in some cases can gain a competitive edge by being at the forefront of the application of technology to support the business.

Make sure your organization takes some of the quality journals about information management. Include yourself on the distribution, and make a point of discussing relevant items or issues with your colleagues (including IT professionals). Suitable journals are *MIS Quarterly, Journal of IT, International Journal of Information Management, Journal of Strategic IT, European Journal of Information Systems*, and (at the detailed level of office systems) *What to Buy for Business. Business Automation* is a useful monthly of abstracts about applications of IT/IS.

Make information management an integral part of your business thinking. Get used to the idea of 'information' as a resource for your business, and IT/IS as a method of handling that resource more effectively. Get into the habit of considering investment in information systems alongside investments in other areas of business activity.

Take a general interest in the use of IT/IS within the organization. Often the use of systems has spread from the bottom up, with computers being used first for operational-level systems such as stock-control, personnel management and accounting packages. Remember that your interest and encouragement is important for the success of new systems, even if you will not be routinely using them yourself.

Where electronic networks are being used as part of office automation, find out what facilities and services are offered, and, if appropriate, arrange to have a terminal in at least the outer office. Where electronic mail (E-mail) is changing the way day-to-day communication and report-writing are done, consider whether you should be on the system, and get at least a basic skill in using it.

The middle manager/user

The organization does not comprise just top managers and IT professionals. The majority of people – thank goodness! – are concerned with the day-to-day operations of the business, and the medium-term management of those operations. They will all use information to do their work and measure their results. This applies whichever primary sector of the economy the business operates in:

(a) *Agriculture and energy.* Here most people are dealing with tangible, or at least measurable, products. Sheep, wheat, gas and electricity output can all be measured. A distribution system is used to deliver the product to the eventual consumer. In the UK in 1989 this sector accounted for only 3.4 per cent of the employed workforce, a figure that had fallen from 4.8 per cent in 1979.

(b) *Manufacturing and construction.* Here again the product is tangible and measurable. Motor cars, hi-fi equipment, buildings and pharmaceutical products are examples. In 1989 27.7 per cent of the UK employed workforce was in this sector, a figure which had fallen from 36.6 per cent in 1979.

(c) *Services.* This sector is expanding rapidly: from 58.6 per cent to 68.9 per cent of the UK employed workforce between 1979 and 1989. This proportion is now typical for advanced economies. It includes such activities as transportation, hairdressing, financial services, wholesale distribution and retail operations. Within this sector, finance is the biggest, and fastest-growing component. All these statistics are taken from official sources (HMSO, 1991).

In all these activities 'information' has a role to play. It is closely bound up with the monitoring and control of other resources which are available to the enterprise: people, money, buildings and plant, energy, and time. From the individual to the corporate level in the organization, we all manage some of these resources, using information to do so.

However, in some types of activity 'information' is relatively more important. For example, the agricultural worker may only need to be told to plough a field to a depth of 30 cm before going off on his tractor to do his day's work. The mechanic on the car production line may need to be told how and where to fit just the one or two components for which he is responsible, and he is ready for another day's pretty boring work. In the service sector information tends to be relatively more important.

For example, in a *hospital* the clinical work is based upon medical knowledge and information, held partly by the clinicians (doctors) themselves but also available in other forms delivered by IT/IS. Expert systems can assist in the diagnosis of particular types of symptom, such as acute abdominal pain, where decisions must be made quickly by busy staff and the implications of error are very serious. The hospital also depends on administrative information systems, to use the beds effectively, to make sure staff with appropriate skills are correctly timetabled, to maximize the use of operating-theatres' and surgeons' time, and to make sure that food, laundry, consumable items and medicines are all in the right place at the right time.

To take another example, in the dealing room of a City *finance house* information is vital to minute-to-minute dealing operations. Information comes over computer and telecommunication systems from external sources, about the money markets, industrial and economic trends, changing consumer requirements, political events and so on. The detailed operations of this enterprise depend upon information to permit good-quality decisions and then rapid implementation of those decisions.

On a smaller scale, an *individual consultant* (on management, law, engineering or any other discipline) is the hub of an information system which uses a wide range of types of information. Some of it is formal (facts about statute law, for example); some of it is informal (knowledge about the style and prejudices of people with whom one must deal, for example). Some is external and some is internal. The consultant uses his distinctive skill to process this information, to add value and produce a report which the client is prepared to pay for. The value of the physical document is usually trivial; it is the information content which has the significant value.

In all these cases information is important. The middle managers of the enterprise need to be conscious of this, think how things could be improved, and seek appropriate IT/IS to help their business activities. It may help if they are already users of IT/IS; if they aren't, then there are the additional barriers of unfamiliarity and lack of awareness of what IT/IS can offer. First, though, they need to consider carefully where 'information' is important in what their business does. Porter and Millar (1985) have offered the idea of information intensity to help in this. Figure 2.2 shows their approach.

Information intensity matrix

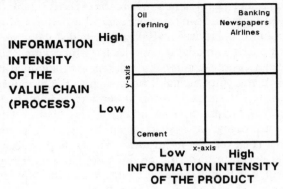

Figure 2.2   *Information intensity. (Derived from Porter and Millar, 1985)*

Ask yourself where 'information' is an important ingredient for your enterprise:

1   In the *product* you sell, whether this is a tangible good or a service (X-axis: low or high).
2   In the *process* by which you make, offer, or deliver the product (Y-axis: low or high).

The answers can give a clue as to where IT/IS might be able to add value, by improving the way information is processed and used. To illustrate this in practice, let's look more closely at three of the examples shown in Figure 2.2 and see how they relate to what has happened in the real world of business.

Use of IT/IS in cement industry

Cement, shown in the Low–Low corner of Figure 2.2, might be considered boring, with little opportunity to add value to either the product or the process by means of IT/IS. However, there are at least two reasons why this is not wholly true:

(a) The *product* (cement) is usually a commodity – something which is widely available, and of which there are several competing producers. Of the three

generic business strategies (cost, differentiation, and niche), most producers therefore have to choose cost as the basis for staying competitive.
They won't sell more cement by putting interesting information on the
bag; consumers know what they are going to use cement for, and don't
need to be told. However, there are two caveats about this. First, there may
be a niche market for special types of cement where the expertise about the
specialist application is scarce, and can therefore add value to the product.
For example, the agricultural fertilizer division of ICI added value to its
commodity product by offering an advisory service to farmers about how
to use the ICI products. Secondly, commodity markets are no longer just
about having the raw commodity available on a shelf in the producer's
premises. Increasingly the customer expects a service: cement to *his*
specification, delivered to *his* premises at a time of *his* choice. Thus
commodity producers need a logistics system which can help differentiate
them from their rivals. For example, a European wholesale producer of
chemical products developed an ordering/production-planning/delivery
information system which within 20 seconds could commit the company
to a requested delivery. This made it possible formally to accept a
customer's order during a telepnone conversation, thus improving the
service, impressing the customer, and leading to greater market share.

(b) The *process* of making cement is a closely controlled and well-understood
chemical activity. However, when operators are given manual control of
the process, they tend, quite naturally, to err on the safe side; they do not
run the process quite near enough to the optimal safe efficiency. Blue Circle
Cement has found that an expert system which encapsulates rules or
knowledge about the production process can control it more efficiently.
Blue Circle installed the system in six production sites. The cost for each
was about £465K, and the saving in energy costs about 500K per year.
Thus the payback period was less than 1 year. The DTI has published video
and case-study examples of this and other applications of expert systems
technology, together with details of the financial benefit to the business in
each case (DTI, 1990).

Use of IT/IS in banking

We are all familiar with the retail banking services of the high-street banks.
The use of automated teller machines (ATMs) and credit/debit cards has
transformed the way we handle money in everyday life. The use of IT/IS has
become fundamental to the way banks do their business, and how they seek to
differentiate their products from those of their competitors. The major banks
are developing customer-oriented database systems, so that each customer
can be given a more personalized service, relevant to his or her needs. In the UK

the First Direct Bank has no traditional branches, but relies on ATM machines, and a 24-hour telephone service to receive customers' instructions. It is developing a niche in the retail banking sector.

Wholesale banking, too, has been changed by IT/IS. Major corporate clients may be given terminals with access to the Bank's software to help them in their financial planning. Decision support systems help evaluate changing market conditions, and optimize investment or the timing of delivery of goods and services. Thus banking has a wholly information-based product, and is increasingly information-intense in the way that product is delivered to the customer.

Airlines' use of IT/IS

Air travel used to be a high-margin, high-value product, protected by government regulation. Recently it has become a commodity market, with certain niches but generally much more competitive. As with cement, the customer no longer wants a take-it-or-leave-it attitude from the supplier; he wants a *service* to meet his travel needs. Thus the airlines compete to provide an added-value service, to include, for example, journey planning, financial arrangements, and hotel, car, and theatre reservations. American Airlines is a classic case of the use of IT for competitive advantage; with IBM it introduced the first effective electronic airline reservation system in the US. The system is called SABRE and gave American Airlines a market lead which it has never lost. Indeed by 1988 it was making more money from SABRE than from flying aeroplanes. Its vice-president (Hopper, 1990) has stated that American Airlines' competitive edge now lies in the creative use of the *information* which its systems can handle, rather than in the *systems* themselves. The company has therefore been able to sell the basic reservation software for useful sums of money, e.g. to the French Railways (SNCF). Thus for airlines, too, information is important in both the product and its production and delivery.

Way ahead for middle managers

These examples from the three sectors of the economy show how 'information' is becoming more important. There is a definite shift towards 'service' as the basis of what an enterprise offers to the market-place, and service is underpinned by the rapid and effective use of information systems. Middle managers and users of such systems should be thinking about their business activity in these terms. It is a matter of viewing IT/IS as something pervasive – woven into the very fabric of the organization. This perspective has much in common with modern thinking about the marketing concept and total quality management (TQM).

The middle manager/user should therefore be increasingly aware of what IT/IS could do to support his part of the business. He naturally expects the appropriate systems to be purchased or developed by the organization, so that he can get on and do a better job. Yet often this simply does not seem to happen. The middle manager/user then feels frustrated by what he sees as bureaucracy and short-sighted parsimony. In desperation he therefore might resort to buying personal computers (PCs), and other low-cost items which can be hidden in the petty cash or other local budgets. He soon discovers, though, that this method has severe limitations. Those PCs which were bought with such high hopes and good intentions don't quite do all that was expected of them. Several people seem only now to realize the cost and time needed to build up databases and try to keep them in step with information elsewhere in the organization. No, IT has been a failure, they conclude.

This is the kind of situation which can develop between middle managers/users and the rest of the organization. So what behaviour should you, as a senior manager, try to cultivate in the middle manager/user? Here are some suitable points of advice for them, which you might like to consider and add to.

As a middle manager, or user of IT/IS, you should:

(a) Think about 'information' as a resource, and how it can contribute to an improved product, and to improved production and delivery of that product to the customer.
(b) Think about how IT/IS could support the handling of this information, to improve the product or the process. Consider what the benefit to the business would be.
(c) Discuss your broad ideas with the appropriate top managers, to see how they fit into broader business strategy, and to ensure that any possible wider application of the ideas is adequately discussed.
(d) Discuss the practicability of your ideas with the IT professionals. You might be expecting something quite unrealistic at the present state of technology, or the cost might be much higher than you expect. Remember that initial hardware and software capital costs are only part of the picture; staff and support costs over the life-cycle of the project can far exceed these initial capital costs.
(e) Be ready to play a full role in working with top managers and IT professionals to see the ideas through to a successful conclusion.

The IT professional

The third corner of the IM triangle shown in Figure 2.1 is the IT professional. Only the smallest firms have no internal IT resource, and have to rely for advice on consultants and vendors. Most medium and large enterprises will have their own IT or IS department (ISD), with its own line-management structure and its own professional head. These are the IT professionals.

What role are the IT professionals playing in your organization at present? Here are some of the undesirable situations which can occur in practice:

(a) The ISD may be a closely knit group that keeps others (including top managers and middle managers/users) at arm's length. They know and love their information systems, which seem to cost more every year. The justification for this expenditure is expressed in obscure quasi-technical language, which Top Managers do not understand but which they hesitate to question.

(b) The senior IT professionals are not very comfortable talking in business language. There seems to be a communication gap between them and top managers when it comes to discussing issues of corporate policy and the business benefit of the investment in IT/IS.

(c) The ISD may have grown up within the first major user-department in the organization. Often this is finance, personnel or stock-control. One part of the business therefore seems to have a monopoly of expertise about IT/IS. Other departments then have difficulty in getting their needs recognized and anything done about them.

(d) At working level the ISD may have a distant relationship with the users of its systems. There is much emphasis on 'the user stating his requirement, so that we can go away and develop systems to meet that requirement'. This attitude can often lead to users without special knowledge trying to think up how IT/IS could help them (or giving up in the attempt); a lengthy backlog of systems development work (often several years); and eventual delivery of systems which are no longer appropriate for the needs of the business, or which were specified by someone who has long since gone. These symptoms indicate a failure of attitude and a failure to take account of technical developments (like fourth-generation languages), which depend on a close co-operation between individual users and the technical support staff.

(e) The IT professionals themselves have difficulty in keeping abreast of technical developments which could be of benefit to the business. You can't entirely blame them for this; the technology is advancing at a remarkable rate (doubling in performance every 3 years or so), and the range of technical and trade publications is daunting. Quite often there is an imbalance of expertise between the two main components of IT: computing and telecommunications. Because the trend is for the integration of computers with telecommunication networks (both local- and wide-area networks), a balance of skills is essential. Quite commonly the computing expertise outweighs the communication expertise.

This may all sound rather depressing, especially if you recognize some of these symptoms among the IT professionals in your organization. However, the symptoms also suggest the type of behaviour which you as a leader in the organization need to cultivate in your IT Professionals, and also bear in mind when recruiting them.

As an IT professional, you should:

(a) Take a close interest in the state and development of the business which your systems are intended to support. Avoid technical jargon when dealing with users and managers, and try to ensure that you and your staff establish sensible discussion with them, at all levels of the organization.

(c) Maintain a broad awareness of the technical developments which could be of value to your business, and keep senior managers appraised of those you think are promising.

(c) Be ready to work with potential users of systems, to help them to develop requirements which make business and technical sense. Use the appropriate technology to develop systems with the full co-operation of users. As far as possible, design systems which are modular or flexible, and which can therefore evolve to meet changing business needs in the future.

Organizational measures

We have looked at the three members of the IM triangle: top managers, middle managers/users, and IT professionals. You may have recognized some of the undesirable symptoms. If you recognize them all, then you and your organization have a serious problem (which you, being a senior manager, will view as an opportunity!). In any case the list of desirable aspects of behaviour will be useful in deciding what you need to do in your particular situation. We shall return to that on page 23, when you will carry out Part 1 of your IM audit. The whole of this book is about the range of measures you need to take if you want to avoid the bitter experience which some organizations have had with IT/IS, and which has lead to the wry saying given in Figure 2.3.

First, then, let's consider some organizational measures which you might take to smooth the working of the IM partnership. Good intentions by individuals are not enough; you need to have the appropriate organizational arrangements in place. We'll look at six policy, structural and organizational measures which modern enterprises are finding useful.

Generic policy for IT/IS

You need a policy framework for IT/IS. This policy will depend upon what business you are in, and could even vary from one part of the business to another. Figure 2.4 provides a way of thinking about this.

2 + 2 = ½

Twice the	Twice the	Half the
time	**budget**	**performance**

Figure 2.3   *The IT/IS formula*

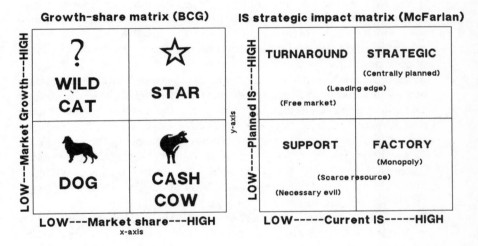

Figure 2.4   *Strategic matrices*

Most managers will be familiar with the left-hand matrix in Figure 2.4. This is the Boston Consulting Group (BCG) matrix, which categorizes products according to their present market-share (X-axis) and the future growth of that market (Y-axis). The four categories of product are shown by their colloquial names: dog, wild cat (or question mark), star, and cash cow. A successful product which survives from a new market through to a mature market will move through those categories in roughly that order. This means that product evolution is clockwise on the diagram, as drawn. A fuller explanation of the BCG matrix is given in standard texts, e.g. MacMillan (1986).

The right-hand matrix was developed by McFarlan *et al.* (1983). It asks you to consider the strategic impact (or importance) of information systems. The X-axis relates to current systems, and the Y-axis relates to future, planned systems. The names in capitals in each of the four boxes are those given by McFarlan as a classification for each situation. The names in brackets are so-called generic policies for the control of IT/IS, relevant to the corresponding part of the matrix; these are described more fully by Remenyi (1988). There is a useful analogy between the boxes of the BCG matrix and the IS strategic impact matrix. Taking the four categories in order:

(a) A *dog* product is bad news: it has a low share of a static market. Unless you can move it quickly to one of the other categories, you will divest it. In management terms, you may be prepared to *support* it reluctantly for a while. You will adopt a *necessary evil* policy towards IT investment relating to this product, approving only what is demonstrably essential in the short term.

(b) A *wild cat* is a bit more encouraging; at least the market is growing. You need to *turnaround* the product to higher market share. For IT, you adopt a *free market*, where local product-managers have to compete for IT resources, and balance them against other resources for the development of their product.

(c) A *star* is good news but needs sustaining. It may have its high market share because of a competitive edge given by IT/IS. This might be to the product itself, the process of making the product, or in the method of delivering the product to the customer; this was discussed on pages 12–15. The market is expanding, and future success will depend on advancing the use of IT/IS. This is the *strategic* situation; the product is important for the future of the business. Use of IT will be *centrally planned*, because it is so closely related to the future success of the star product and therefore to business strategy. The stakes are higher than in the wild cat case.

(d) The *cash cow* is the strong, mature and profitable product. It provides cash to finance the development of new or more uncertain products. The operation tends to be large-scale and stable, like a *factory*. The use of IT is arranged as a *monopoly*: centrally controlled for that operation, with local or junior managers having little option in the matter.

Few businesses today have the stability of a dependable cash cow which will assure their profitability for years ahead. Most businesses have to fight for market share, and plan a portfolio of products which will reach their peak profitability in turn. For them a single generic policy for IT/IS will not be appropriate.

This is a vital point for senior managers to appreciate. The policy for IT/IS needs to be matched not only to the situation of the business as a whole, but to the situation and classification of its individual products or activities. Where the business is organized into product divisions, this may be quite straightforward for you to organize. Where you need several policies for different parts of one division, it can be more difficult. In any case there is likely to be moaning and comparisons; you need to be able to explain the business rationale for the policy you are adopting in each particular case.

The IT/IS steering committee

The generic policy defines the framework for IT/IS in the organization. It is worth you considering some related but more detailed issues. The IT/IS steering committee is a method of getting senior managers to play their part in IT/IS, at an appropriate policy level but without taking an unreasonable amount of their time. The steering committee will be the authority for the information strategy document, which links business policy and policy for IT/IS, defines the organizational arrangements for IT/IS (based on the generic policy), and defines broad policy for systems, e.g. hardware, software and architecture policy. The committee should usually be chaired by a senior non-IT business manager (usually a director). It should meet at least quarterly, and more often if major changes or projects are afoot. It should act as the overseeing body, balancing the considerations of IT professionals and users, within the framework of business needs. It is the visible evidence of an effective IM partnership at senior level.

Joint project teams

These ensure that IT professionals and middle-managers/users work closely together in the development of individual large projects. The old model of the system development process was for users to state requirements, IT professionals to go away and design and implement systems, and then for them to deliver the systems formally to the user. With today's pressing timescales, and the nature of modern system development tools, this model is no longer appropriate. There must be a much more integrated and parallel set of activities. We shall look at this more closely in Chapter 6, but the management point here is to have closely integrated teams of users and IT professionals, preferably co-located. A joint project team should report progress regularly to the IT/IS steering committee. Earl (1989) has developed the idea of 'teams and themes' for the succcessful implementation of IT/IS; there are many facets to the project and complementary skills and contributions are needed.

Decentralized IS departments

The bulk of the work of an ISD is usually concerned with maintenance of systems: providing user-support and advice, investigating failures of hardware or software, undertaking minor modifications and development. In all these respects it must work closely with users in various departments of the business. Many enterprises are now decentralizing the ISD to make it work more effectively. A decision to do this should of course relate to the business organization generally; autonomous divisions will most likely need their own IT resource, but should make their own decision as to how centralized or decentralized that should be internally. The trend, though, is now towards decentralizing as far as you can, while retaining a coherent overall policy (the information strategy).

Businessmen running IS departments

As a senior manager, you should try to get rid of some of the mystique about IT/IS. Of course it is a highly technical subject with its own terminology and jargon, but this is no excuse for obfuscation. Many enterprises are now putting businessmen in charge of the ISD, to improve the dialogue with top management and to bring sound business principles to bear within the ISD. This can be particularly important if you are going to follow the trend towards running the ISD as a cost- or profit-centre, with service level agreements (SLAs) with its customers inside (and possibly outside) the organization. Business managers must of course have some affinity and interest in the IT function, but an independent, non-specialist mind can bring refreshing change to ISDs which may have got stuck in a rut.

Growing 'hybrid managers'

This is a related issue. The term 'hybrid manager' was coined at the end of the 1980s to describe a manager who was equally comfortable dealing with business matters and with matters of IT policy and implementation. They tend to be rare. In 1986 a general manager of Barclays Bank said there were 4,000 IT professionals in the bank, but of these only seven were what he would call hybrids. Since then there have been conscious efforts to 'grow' hybrids, within the organization and with external training courses. The development and progression of these hybrids should be a concern of senior managers in any organization for which IT/IS is of major business significance. They have a pivotal role in helping senior management keep an overview of the place and the potential of IT/IS in the business. As part of this, they may need to use one of the growth models for IT/IS. A recent development of growth models has been made by Galliers (1991), for example.

Taking stock

This chapter has been about establishing an information management partnership in your enterprise. A simple but useful model to consider is the IM triangle: top managers, middle managers/users, and the IT professionals. We have considered the characteristics, both undesirable and desirable, for each. Finally, we have looked at the policy and organizational arrangements to encourage effective co-operation, once the individual will is there.

Rather than make a detailed summary of the points, I now invite you to carry out the first part of the IM audit for your organization. The format and method of scoring were explained on page 6, and the ten questions for Part 1 are shown in Figure 2.5.

Guideline: Establish an information management partnership			
Ser.	Question	Score	Action
1	Is there effective communication between all members of the IM triangle?		
2	Are top managers reluctant to take up IT/IS?		
3	Do top managers relate IT/IS to their business thinking?		
4	Do middle managers/users assess information in product and process?		
5	Do middle managers/users get a sympathetic response to their needs?		
6	Do the senior IT professionals understand the business?		
7	Do the IT professionals work closely with users, to apply IT well?		
8	Do you have a generic policy for IT/IS, related to the business?		
9	Do you have the necessary formal arrangements to control IT/IS?		
10	Are you growing hybrids in the organization?		
	TOTALS		

Figure 2.5 *IM audit – Part 1*

Think about the questions, answer them honestly, and make a note of any special points that occur to you from each.

References

DTI (1990), 'Expert System Opportunities: Case Studies, Guidelines, and Video Pack', HMSO, for Department of Trade and Industry, London.

Earl, M. J. (1989), *Management Strategies for Information Technology*, Prentice-Hall.

Galliers, R. D. (1991), 'Strategic Information Systems planning: myths, reality and guidelines for successful implementation', *Eur. J. Inf. Sys*, Vol. 1, No. 1, pp. 55–64.

HMSO (1991), *Britain – An Official Handbook*, HMSO, London.

Hopper (1990), 'Rattling SABRE – New Ways to Compete on Information', *Harvard Business Review*, Vol. 68, No. 3, pp. 118–25 (May–June).

McFarlan, F. W. *et al.* (1983), 'The Information Archipelago – plotting a course', *Harvard Business Review*, Vol. 61, No. 1, pp. 145–56 (Jan.–Feb.).

MacMillan, K. (1986), 'Strategy: Portfolio Analysis', *Journal of General Management*, Vol. 11, No. 4, pp. 94–112.

Porter, M. E. and Millar, V. E. (1985), 'How Information gives you Competitive Advantage', *Harvard Business Review*, Vol. 63, No. 4, pp. 149–60 (July–Aug.).

Remenyi, D. S. J. (1988), *Increase Profits with Strategic Information Systems*, NCC Publications.

3 The generic benefits of IT/IS

Introduction

The second of the six guidelines for information management is 'Distinguish the potential benefits of IT/IS'. This asks you to be aware of the broad, generic benefits which IT/IS can offer your business. You need to take such a view, related to your own business situation, before you consider specific systems and benefits in more detail.

In Chapter 1 we identified the three generic benefits of IT/IS as efficiency, effectiveness and strategic advantage (or competitive edge). Let's consider what these categories mean in the management context.

As a manager your main concern is to get business results. Of course 'business' here is taken in the widest sense, to include both profit-seeking and non-profit-seeking enterprises, from both the public and the private sector. The 'results' may be expressed in financial terms or by some other measure. Nevertheless a useful broad definition of your work is:

Managers direct **Resources** to achieve **Results**

The resources available to you will include people, money, material, energy, time and information. For each of them the modern world is changing:

- *People*. People are the most important resource of any enterprise. However, people's expectations and the nature of the workforce are changing. Demographic and other social changes are making the long-term, full-time job the exception rather than the rule. Part-time work, working from home, women returning to careers after having children, a greater proportion of older workers, the contracting-out of certain functions, job mobility, and an emphasis on closer team-working are familiar features of modern human-resource management.

- *Money*. This must be the next most important resource. In an increasingly competitive world it is not just a matter of making enough money. It is necessary to make the right amount of money, at the right time, to meet the requirements of more complex cash-flow and investment plans, and to provide some resilience against unforeseen difficulties. Growth and decline in business bring distinct financial problems: growth can mean revenue but no cash; decline can mean cash but no revenue.

- *Material*. Buildings, offices, furniture, machinery, computers, raw stock, and work-in-progress all represent physical assets which are there for a purpose but unless used properly will bring no benefit to the business. Each of these, and many more, have to be controlled and used to good effect. There is increasing pressure to reduce the levels of material assets, to reduce working capital as well as to reduce direct overheads. We see leasing of buildings, hiring of plant and office equipment, tighter control of stock levels, and a closer financial control of cash-flow in step with the movement of raw materials and finished products.

- *Energy*. Energy is similar. It is getting more expensive. We are rightly more concerned now about the environmental implications of our demand for energy, and our tendency to waste it. We therefore need to manage energy in all its forms, to reduce waste and to get better results from what we do consume. International events point to the fragility of many of our assumptions about the continued availability of cheap energy. Scientific knowledge about global warming, acid rain and other environmental dangers lead us to seek 'sustainable growth' of the economy rather than just 'growth' for its own sake.

- *Time*. This is an odd one. Time is unlike the other resources – you can't buy more of it. In reality you have to manage within the constraints of time; it waits for no man. Nevertheless we speak of 'time management', at both the personal and the corporate level; we really mean the planning and adjustment of other activities to achieve best results within the available time constraints. Project management, and its supporting techniques such as PERT/CPA, are all about this. The pressures on an individual's time, and upon corporate time, always seem to increase. It is a paradox of advanced economies that we have some people who are short of time, overworked and under stress as a result; a minority who have too much time, are under-employed or unemployed and under a different stress as a result; and a majority who appear to have a higher standard of living with increased leisure and other opportunities. Which category does time constrain you to?

- *Information*. This is even odder, as mentioned in the preface. It is intangible, subjective, and difficult to assign a financial value to. Its value often depends on its timeliness for a particular purpose. Nevertheless, information is bound up with the control and management of all the other resources. It is also a commodity in its own right: you can buy facts and figures from the outside world, add value to them by processing or fresh presentation, and then perhaps sell them to the outside world in this value-added form. The pervasive nature of information, as a management resource, explains why IT/IS, by improving the handling of information, can have such a major impact on the enterprise. Information is certainly becoming more important as a management resource; the economic trends mentioned in Chapter 2 are evidence of that.

IT/IS continues to expand at a remarkable rate, with the processing power doubling every 3 years, and costs coming down at the same time. The cost of most other resources is going up, while this one is coming down. That in itself is reason to give it careful management attention. The elusive nature of information, and the determination of executive information requirements, are addressed, for example, by Galliers (1987).

In this chapter we shall look in turn at the three generic benefits of IT/IS, and illustrate them with practical examples. The thirty examples and their classification are summarised in Figure 3.2. They will provide a backcloth for the ideas later in the book: you will be able to judge them against the examples as well as your own experience. The broad distinction between the generic benefits is as follows:

1 *Efficiency* is about saving other resources, by doing the same job better than the way you did it before. This reduces *costs*.
2 *Effectiveness* is about making other resources more effective, by doing a better job than the one you did before. This improves the *return on assets* (RoA) for those other resources.
3 *Strategic advantage* (or competitive *edge*) is about changing some aspect of what the business does. We can call it 'systems-intensive business development' – bettering the business in a way which is underpinned by the use of IT/IS. Developing the business in this way will result in *growth* (shown by an increase in revenue, profit or throughput, depending on how you measure business performance in your particular case).

These generic benefits are illustrated in Figure 3.1.

We shall develop this figure later in the chapter, but there are a few points to make at the outset. The generic benefits are not watertight compartments; practical systems often cover more than one of them. For example, a system may offer some immediate savings *and* release spare capacity to make the operation more effective or to enable the business to grow. The management context and intention are as important as the visible system itself. Thus you, as a senior manager, must decide, or agree, the management motivation for each system in your enterprise. You will then be clear what type of benefits are being sought, and how you will know whether they are being achieved.

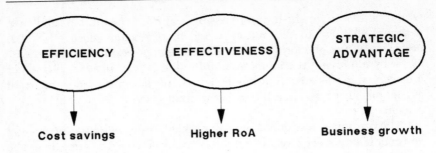

Figure 3.1 *Generic benefits – 1*

The three categories make a useful distinction, which will become even more important when we consider specific benefits. Let's now look at practical examples of how IT/IS can offer the three generic benefits. Think about the examples, in the context of Figure 3.1, and try to see which features are similar to your own experience or current situation.

Systems for efficiency

'Efficiency' systems save other resources, and hence reduce costs. This was the most obvious application for computing technology when it became widely available in the 1960s. Let's look at some practical examples of how businesses have used IT/IS to give efficiency benefits, to give savings of people, money, material, energy or time.

People

Many of the early mainframe systems were concerned with automating detailed business processes, and thus saving the human clerks who had previously done the same job with paper-based procedures. Examples are accounting, stock-control, personnel records and similar operational-level systems. Saving people was the main motive. There may still be scope for this in your business, but most companies are moving on to the other benefits.

An example of this progression is the Friends Provident insurance company in the UK. In the late 1970s it introduced a system called GLADIS to its branch offices; this automated the firm's internal transactions, to make them more efficient. In 1982 it used one of the public viewdata (videotex) systems to link in the firm's brokers and agents; this was called FRENTEL. It made some savings possible, but also gave capacity to expand the business. Over a 9-year period the business (measured in terms of new life-insurance policies per member of staff) increased four-fold, while the volume of business increased by a similar amount. Thus what might originally have been seen as just an internal efficiency system began to give both effectiveness and strategic benefits. It enabled the company to grow (partly by takeover) to achieve a better business position without major increase in the number of people.

A second example is the computer manufacturer Digital Equipment Corporation – DEC. It developed an expert system which would help to design a configuration of its equipment to meet each customer's requirements. Previously this had required much detailed work by skilled and knowledgeable people. The system reduced the requirement for these skilled and expensive people.

The third example is from the public sector. The UK Department of Social Security (DSS) is responsible for approving and paying benefits to people who are unemployed, disabled, or have other special claims. The rules for this are very complex and the DSS had to train large numbers of people to administer benefits and deal with individual members of the public. This, in turn, made that group of workers quite powerful; they could demand extra pay for their skills and take industrial action to support this.

The DSS developed a system which would give an authoritative statement of eligibility for benefits when the factual details of a particular case were fed in. This meant greater accuracy and consistency of the decisions made. When the rules are changed (as administrative rules tend to be), then it is a matter of changing the software once, not retraining or updating large numbers of people. The DSS thus became less dependent on this one group of people. There is a downside, of course; the individuals might view their jobs as deskilled, and might therefore become demotivated.

Money

The retail banks now operate large networks of automated teller machines (ATMs, or cash-points). Their original motive for this was to save on human staff (tellers) who were spending much of their time serving customers on simple transactions like withdrawal of cash. In fact some of the banks found that the greater benefit from ATMs arose from the consequent changes in the way customers managed their bank accounts. With the greater convenience of withdrawing cash, customers were taking out smaller amounts of cash, but more often. This left a higher average balance in the account, which the bank was then free to invest (at a higher rate than the interest they had to pay to the customer).

In the public sector there is a system for assessing individual entitlements to retirement pensions. The manual system was very labour-intensive, and was replaced by an expert system which could apply the many complex rules to individual cases. The financial cost of running the system was reduced by about £1m per year. At the same time the accuracy increased from 90 per cent to 100 per cent and the response time reduced from about 3 months to around 10 days. Thus there was a package of benefits, of which the financial saving had the most immediate impact. The other benefits were in the quality of service to the public. This is important, but public-sector managers are often under heavy pressure to make financial savings as a first priority. A monopoly situation (which the public sector often has) places a special discipline and responsibility upon the manager, because he lacks many of the pressures of market forces.

Material

All businesses have tangible resources, such as buildings, which need to be managed efficiently. However, manufacturing enterprises have the additional material assets of their factories, raw stock, and work-in-progress. This represents working capital which produces no immediate return to the business. UK industry has an estimated £40b worth of stock in hand, and a typical factory is adding value to that material for only 15 per cent of the time. If this figure could be raised to just 50 per cent, then there could be a three-fold reduction in stockholdings. IT/IS can help, by implementing just-in-time (JIT) and Kanban procedures. These terms are explained in, for example, Kempner (1987). One way to do this is for a factory to have materials resource planning (MRP) computer systems, and electronic data interchange (EDI) links with its suppliers, so that the ordering and supply of raw materials or components can be much more tightly controlled, and related to the needs of the production facility. The Rover Group estimates that the use of EDI can cut £200 off the cost of a car – an important saving in a competitive mass-market.

An even more striking example is Benetton, Italy's largest sports- and fashion-wear manufacturer. It has no production facilities of its own; all production is sub-contracted. Moreover it reduces inventory by only producing against orders in hand; this is important in a fast-changing fashion market. It uses a value added network (VAN) to interconnect the computer systems, and has thus been able to rationalize the number of its direct sub-contractors.

Energy

On pages 13–14 we saw how Blue Circle Cement was able to save £3m per year in energy costs by an expert system which controlled its cement kilns more efficiently. The energy consumption was reduced by 3–4 per cent by running the kilns closer to ideal conditions, based on best expertise made available through the expert system.

There are huge opportunities for saving energy, outside of specialist production facilities like Blue Circle's. Official estimates are that the UK is already achieving £500m per year of *energy-saving* through efficiency measures, but it could save at least £7.6b per year (20 per cent of energy costs). See HMSO (1991). IT has a major part in this, with telemetry, monitoring, planning and control systems linked together electrically. Energy-saving systems can be introduced to improve existing installations, or as part of new buildings.

Time

Computers may be stupid, but they are certainly fast! Systems have been used to speed up business operations where time is an important aspect. In the US American Hospital Supply is a wholesale supplier of medical goods. In 1978 it introduced its automated system for analytical purchasing, or ASAP. Even the acronym (which usually stands for 'as soon as possible') suggests what the benefit will be. The company provided free terminals for its customers (hospitals), at which staff could enter the orders electronically. This proved quick and convenient, compared with the paper-based procedures. Time, and costs, for the hospitals were reduced, while the size of the average order increased because staff found the system more convenient. By 1987 sales had grown by 17 per cent per year, market share was over 50 per cent, and the firm's profits were four times the industry average. This example is often quoted as a strategic use of IT, but the benefit originally lay in the time-saving, both to the customer and to American Hospital Supply.

Another example where time saved meant more business was Federal Express (Fed-Ex). In the 10 years to 1983 Fred Smith, the founder, grew Fed-Ex to become a $1b business. To achieve overnight delivery, Fed-Ex in the US have three regional computer centres, VDUs in their lorries, and bar-codes on individual items. This system keeps track of the progress of each item, to achieve assured delivery and provide evidence of it. Other transportation systems (air, road and sea) use remote data-monitoring to check the position and state of the goods in transit. Unloading operations and onward transmission can then be planned in detail well before the cargo arrives.

Systems for effectiveness

The management intention behind an 'effectiveness' system is not to make immediate savings but to make other resources more effective. It is not just about doing the same job better; it is about doing a better job. This should increase the return on assets (RoA) for those other resources, and may in turn give scope for growing or improving the business, as shown in Figure 3.1.

People

We'll take three examples of how IT/IS can make people more effective. The first is FI Group, a software development company which achieves its mission by 'developing, through modern telecommunications, the unutilized intellectual energy of individuals and groups unable to work in a conventional environment'. Most of the Group's employees are women working flexibly at home, using a PC terminal. There are also local work-centres, which provide some social element to the job without incurring the heavy cost of commuting (money, time and nervous energy). Most of FI's people would not be able to work in any other way, but this aspect does not interfere with the FI product: it is a software house, competing with other software houses in the same market.

The second example is the ICI Plant Protection Division. It had a sales team who visited farmers. First the Division used viewdata systems to improve control of the team, most of whom were based at home. Then it developed an advisory expert system which the salespeople could use on laptop computers when giving advice to farmers. This improved the farmers' awareness and perception of the company and its products, increased its profile and kept competition at bay. The sales team was not disbanded; it became more effective in sustaining, and then growing, the business.

In the US the General Electric Company (GE) had to deal with customers using a very wide range of its products. It was impossible for a single person to know enough about all the products to respond intelligently to all possible types of enquiry from members of the public. So GE centralized its customer enquiry system in the US, and gave rapid computer assistance to the staff. This made them more effective in their job, and also meant that GE was able to build up much more detailed data about the performance of its products in the market.

Money

The money markets use IT/IS to make more effective use of the money which passes through their control. During the 1980s dealing changed from paper-based to electronic systems, and today the dealers compete on the quality and speed of the decisions they make. They therefore make extensive use of IT/IS for decision support systems (DSS), which can identify attractive courses of action (such as arbitrage, where a sequence of exchanges can produce a net profit) and make recommendations to the dealer. Because these systems often give a competitive edge, there is often a reluctance to divulge details.

A second example is where banks offer their major corporate clients investment advisers, from terminals linked into the bank's own system. The benefit is that the client can improve his investment management, faster than before, without consulting the bank on all the details.

Material

Today building management is a complex matter, with several timescales for various aspects:

(a) *Shell*. This is the basic structure of the building, and is usually designed for a 50-year life.
(b) *Services*. Heating, ventilating and air-conditioning (HVAC) services have a 15-year life.
(c) *Scenery*. This refers to partitioning, office equipment and the like, and may have a life of 5–7 years.
(d) *Set*. This means the arrangement of facilities to meet immediate needs, and can change daily.

The term 'intelligent building' has been coined to cover the application of IT/IS in all these aspects. At present the market to retro-fit advanced systems into existing shells is larger than the market related to the construction of new shells. HVAC, cable-management, office automation, computer installations and telecommunication systems can all make the building more effective.

A quite different example is S R Gent, a clothing manufacturer. Most of its output goes to the Marks & Spencer retail chain. In this highly competitive market, S R Gent has remained successful by using IT to get efficiency benefits (so that it can compete on cost with the overseas competition) and then seeking to increase its responsiveness to the changing market. It controls the production facilities by real-time information about the sale of its products in the Marks & Spencer stores. At first this had to be done by a senior executive visiting representative stores to judge how well sales were going. Now, though, point of sale (POS) data is collected by the retailer to show what is sold, when, and in which store. However, this data belongs to the retailer, and it is his business judgement whether he is prepared to share it with his wholesale suppliers or not. Use of POS data improves response time and avoids the production of clothing which either will not sell or would take an uneconomic time to sell.

Energy

We have mentioned energy-saving in buildings, but there is a wider aspect to this. Combined heat and power (CHP) schemes can make power-generation systems more effective by using heat which would otherwise be wasted. Alternatively, electrical power can be generated as a by-product of a heating scheme. Power produced in this way can be used by the organization itself, or, in the liberalized market for electrical energy, sold into that market. There are now 500 CHP plants in the UK, producing about 3 per cent of total electricity demands (see HMSO, 1991). The CHP process is complex and needs close computer control, both in respect of the heating and power-generation functions.

A different facet of the energy question is the possible trade-off between using energy to move physical goods and using IT/IS to move information instead. As energy becomes more expensive and IT/IS becomes cheaper, you need to watch this balance. There is an example from the newspaper industry. In the US the Dow Jones company publishes the *Wall Street Journal*. It pioneered national newspapers in the US (which were previously uneconomic due to transport costs) by using electronic transmission of composed pages to seventeen printing plants. This later developed into a global network, with five originating plants and twelve printing plants. The circulation increased substantially.

Time

If your car has broken down and you have telephoned for help, then there is only one criterion of service you have: speed of response. The Automobile Association (AA) is one of the major motoring organizations in the UK. To compete in what was becoming a more competitive market, it needed to improve the response-time of its patrol vehicles to calls from the motorist. It installed a centralized command and control system to do this. First it centralized the control and allocation of resources, based wholly on electronic systems instead of paperwork. Then it provided radio data-links to the patrol vehicles so that the details of jobs and their completion could be exchanged between the control point and the patrolmen in the vehicles. In this way the response time was shortened and the use of existing resources made more effective.

Time was important for a different reason for the management consultancy Peat Marwick McLintock. It needed to speed up the response to clients' enquiries, so that it stood a better chance of being successful in the process of competitive tendering. An office automation system enabled it to develop and authorize response documents much more quickly, and this gave the firm a strategic advantage in its market-place. This and other recent cases in the UK are discussed by Remenyi (1990).

Systems for strategic advantage

The third generic benefit is about improving the business, through 'systems-intensive business development'. There are many ways of doing this, for example:

(a) Using IT/IS to add value to the product, to improve or differentiate it.
(b) Using IT/IS to deliver or support the product.
(c) Using IT/IS to capture new types of information, to improve the quality of management decision-making.
(d) Selling information, or IT/IS, into a new market.

It is all about *new* ways of doing *new* business, not just doing present business better. Let's consider some practical examples which illustrate these four approaches.

Product added-value

The finance sector, because it is wholly information-based, has many examples of new products supported by IT/IS. Home banking is one. In the UK this was pioneered by the Bank of Scotland and the Nottingham Building Society in 1982.

They used the cheap technology of viewdata (the combination of a TV monitor with a telephone line, controlled by a keypad). Using a special terminal, customers can check their bank account, and give instructions over the viewdata system at any time they choose. What emerged was that many people choose to arrange their finances late on a Saturday evening, when there was nothing left to watch on the TV! The serious point is that it often takes a new facility to disclose what is the customer's real preference; it is too easy to assume that 'there is no demand'. So far, home banking has remained a small niche, partly because the viewdata system in the UK still only reaches about one quarter of 1 per cent of households. In France the corresponding Minitel/Teletel system reaches about a quarter of French households; this represents a good customer base, and supports about 12,000 different value-added services. In the absence of such an information infrastructure, you have to resort to the basic telephone service, which reaches 85–90 per cent of households. For home banking it is possible to use 'bleeper-boxes' to send data, or use human operators available at all times, as in the First Direct Bank, which has ATMs but no conventional branches.

A second example of adding value to the product is Buick, a US car manufacturer. It developed an electronic product information center (EPIC) which was installed in its dealers' premises to give information (facts, figures and pictures) about Buick's and competitors' products. There was a new approach to helping the customer identify his need more clearly, and telling him how it could be satisfied. The service was extended to include second-hand cars, meeting the specification as closely as possible. The system would tell the customer where the car was, the extent to which it met his requirements, and how soon it could be delivered. This is an example of adding value to the marketing service which the customer would normally expect. Service is not just about satisfying the customer; it is about surprising the customer and delighting him. IT/IS can help.

Product delivery and support

The Buick example is about marketing through existing outlets, but with an added-value service. Information systems can create new outlets, or electronic markets in their own right. Such electronic markets are becoming important in many areas of business; the issues are addressed by Malone *et al.* (1989). For example, public networks such as viewdata (videotex) are used by insurance brokers to access the computers of insurance companies, to get quotations for individual customer requirements. The broker is thus in a position to compare, on-screen and in the presence of his client, what the various companies can offer. This has strengthened the position of the customer, and increased the competition within that market. If you were a supplier of insurance, you could not afford to ignore such an electronic market, even though it might mean a cut in the profit margins you were used to.

Such an electronic market-place can become a business in its own right. In the US a company called AT&T Transtech was formed in 1983 to provide account and financial services for 22 million AT&T (telephone company) shareholders. This operation developed into a direct-marketing operation. Each year Transtech handles about 22m telephone calls, 140m items of mail, and 150m computer transactions. The operation offers novel features and is very market-driven.

Transtech uses state-of-the-art IT to link voice and data systems. For example, the operator's response to an incoming telephone call will be prompted in a way which varies through the working day and at weekends. Where necessary, the call can be routed quickly to an appropriate specialist. There is rapid access to data about individual and corporate accounts, so that a sensible and detailed response is possible. Transtech takes advantage of new technical advances, such as the integrated services digital network (ISDN). ISDN is the evolving high-speed all digital communication system which is becoming an important opportunity for business telecommunications. It can offer calling-line identification, which gives an electronic indication of the caller's number before the call is answered. Transtech can link this to its database, so that details of the customer's account are on the operator's screen as soon as the call is answered. This saves time and money, and enhances the service to the customer. An ordering and accounting system like this can be offered as a market-place for many types of wholesale producer. Wholesalers are currently under severe pressure from the major retailers, who have the advantage of knowing the market in close detail (through point of sale systems, for example). Thus electronic markets could shift the industry power-balance in several sectors; in this sense they are truly strategic! The AT&T Transtech case is described in more detail by Cobbin *et al.* (1989).

In the UK *Thomson Holidays* created an electronic market for its package-holiday products. Travel agents used to phone into ten reservation centres, which could become overloaded and slow to respond. In 1976 a system to give travel agents access to a complete list of available holidays was introduced. In 1981 the strategic importance of electronic reservation systems had become apparent: one of the travel operators, Sealink, had given 3,500 viewdata terminals to travel agents. So in 1982 Thomson introduced its TOPS on-line reservation system. In 6 weeks it trained 9,000 travel agents' staff to use the terminals, and the system became the industry standard. Thomson became the market leader, with more than 30 per cent market share.

TOPS is designed to deal with the heavy peak of demand which occurs when the new Thomson holiday brochure is issued each year. On the day of issue up to 200,000 reservations can be processed. The system saved Thomson £20–25m per year, but productivity tripled in the period 1978–86; this is another indication of the way the generic benefits are 'mixed' in practical systems. The deputy managing director of Thomson Holidays put it very simply: 'We buy beds and airline seats, and we put them together and market a holiday package. Apart from computer systems, Thomson Holidays owns very little'. Thomson also use a PC-based system to do detailed comparison between its own products and the products of its competitors when the latter issue their brochures; this 'has replaced a pricing cudgel with a scalpel'. TOPS has been a major factor in Thomson Holidays' success. There is an analogy with American Airlines, whose computer-based reservation business now makes more profit than its basic business of flying aeroplanes.

Information capture

The more you know about the outside world, the market in which you operate, and the needs of your customers, the better equipped you are to make sound management decisions. This is very obvious, but it is even more important when the scene is changing rapidly. Let's see how IT/IS has enabled organizations to acquire that wider range of outside information.

McKesson is a wholesale supplier to US chemists' shops (pharmacies or drugstores). In the mid–1970s its customers were feeling the competitive pressure from the larger retail outlets. In order to resist the downward trend, McKesson developed a stock-ordering system which it felt would be attractive to its customers – the small-town chemists. They gave hand-held terminals free to the chemists, who could then walk around their storerooms, see what was needed, and enter the detail into the terminal. Overnight the data would be passed by telephone connection to the McKesson computer system as an order. The order would then be made up and delivered to the chemist.

That much was fairly obvious, and there are parallels with what other suppliers did at that time to 'lock-in' their customers. However, the important point is what McKesson did after it had reaped the immediate benefits of easier order-entry. It was able to build up data about the requirements and consumption of individual chemists. Thus in due course it was able to offer a stock-management service tailored to the needs of each chemist. This was attractive to the chemists, who after all were professional pharmacists and for whom stock-control was just a boring chore of business. McKesson's stock-control and supply service thus became a broader business, made possible by the building up of detailed data about individual customers. McKesson was then able to broaden its scope, to include such items as wine and flowers as well as medical goods. The company became market-leader in the supply business, and, as a sideline, a major processor of medical insurance claims.

Another illustration is the Otis Elevator Company, which supplies elevators (lifts) for buildings. Like the General Electric Company (see page 32), it decided to centralize its customer interface nationally. In the Otis case, the telephone in the elevator could connect to this central Otis facility; this would be invaluable for people stuck in an elevator, or for the reporting of less serious faults. Once this electronic link existed, Otis realized that it could be used to monitor the state of health of the elevator. A self-monitoring device continuously checks the performance of the elevator, and in many cases is able to send a diagnosis and warning to Otis before the fault becomes apparent to the user. This enables Otis to plan preventative maintenance more effectively, and reduces the incidence of faults which directly affect the customer.

There is a common lesson from the McKesson and Otis cases. Once the electronic links have been established with the outside world (particularly with the customer), then you need to look carefully for new types of business opportunity. This has been called 'planning the encore', i.e. to follow your first initiative, and enables you to sustain your competitive advantage. We shall examine the dynamics of this more closely in Chapter 4.

Selling information, or IT/IS

Information can be a commodity in its own right. IT/IS developed for a company's needs may have a market value elsewhere. These two facts indicate possible strategic opportunities which managers need to consider. Let's look at one example of each.

In the UK a full census (survey) of the population is done every 10 years. The most recent was in April 1991. The 1991 census covered some 23 million households, and all the data is being processed on a single mainframe computer, at Titchfield. This will produce summary results by mid–1992 and the final output, comprising some 3,000 tables, by late 1993. The census data is overwhelming in volume, but contains detail which is very valuable for marketing purposes. There is a database called *ACORN* (A Classification Of Residential Neighbourhoods), which is based upon the census data and provides a profile of each of the census enumeration areas (of about 150 dwellings). The occupants are characterized by age, sex, size of household and employment sector. The dwellings are characterized by thirty-eight neigh-bourhood types, ranging from agricultural villages to private flats for single pensioners. More detail is in, for example, Parkinson and Parkinson (1987). The ACORN data is based upon publicly available sources, but is of great commercial value in the targeting of marketing efforts such as direct-mail. The added value lies in the classification scheme, designed for specific business purposes, and in the processing of the data into a manageable form.

For an example of selling IT/IS we can recall the American Airlines case, where the software of the reservation system was sold to SNCF (French Railways), once it was clear that this would not compromise the Airline's competitive advantage. A UK example is provided by Istel, which started as the IT/IS division within British Leyland, the motor manufacturer which was later renamed the Rover Group. The division developed an electronic mail and data communication system, interactive modelling systems, and visual present-ation techniques appropriate to the needs of a motor manufacturer. The company then realized that there was an opportunity to sell these products and services elsewhere in the industry, and then eventually into the public market. In 1984 it adopted the name Istel, to indicate this wider role. In 1987 there was a management buyout from the Rover Group for £35m. One thousand of the 1,400 employees became shareholders. They now operate one of the major UK EDI networks, to meet the needs of Rover Group and others. By 1988 their turnover had reached £84m, with more than half from outside the Rover Group. By 1989 the turnover was £110m, and there was a £180m takeover of the company by AT&T. The Istel case illustrates how a functional IT/IS division can become a profitable business in its own right, and grow at a faster rate than the parent company from which it sprang. Where such opportunities exist, they will affect the policy for managing the ISD, which we discussed in Chapter 2.

Practical points

In this chapter we have looked briefly at thirty case examples of how IT/IS can give the three generic benefits. Figure 3.2 reminds you of the cases, and shows the categories under which we considered them.

Management resource	EFFICIENCY	EFFECTIVENESS	STRATEGIC ADVANTAGE
People	Friends Provident DEC DSS Benefits	FI Group ICI Plant Protection General Electric Co.	1. Product added-value Home Banking Buick (EPIC)
Money	Retail banks: ATMs Retirement pensions	Money markets Investment advisers	2. Product delivery and support AT&T Transtech
Material	Rover: JIT/EDI Benetton	Building management S R Gent	Thomson Holidays 3. Information capture
Energy	Blue Circle Cement Energy-saving	Combined heat/power Dow Jones	McKesson Otis Elevator 4. Selling information, or IT/IS
Time	American Hosp. Supply Federal Express	Automobile Association Peat Marwick McLintock	ACORN Istel

Figure 3.2 *Case examples*

There is a deliberate reason for looking at so many examples this early in the book, and asking you to relate them to your own experience. It is to provide you with some real-life evidence about the use of IT/IS, against which you can judge the guidelines and ideas we shall be discussing throughout the book. Most managers like to start from experience (whether their own or someone else's), and then broaden their thinking into general principles which they can then relate to real problems before deciding what to do.

Of course we have already introduced a simple classification system:

1 The three *generic benefits*: efficiency, effectiveness and strategic advantage.
2 The five *management resources* which may be saved by 'efficiency' systems or improved by 'effectiveness' systems: people, money, material, energy and time.

3   The four *approaches to strategic advantage*: adding value to the product, improving its delivery and support, capturing information, and selling information or IT/IS.

There are three practical points to make about what we have covered in this chapter. First, the benefit classification system, like any other management classification, is not very precise. It can best be considered as a checklist or agenda, for you to use in considering the options. It will suggest various viewpoints, and make sure you don't miss something important.

The case examples themselves don't fit neatly or exclusively into the categories. Indeed in several cases other benefits were more significant. However, there *are* aspects of each case which *do* illustrate the distinctive feature of each category, and that was the reason for using them.

Finally, we have seen several examples, such as Friends Provident, McKesson and Istel, where the flavour of the benefits changed as the system and the business developed. This is very important. As a manager you need to be aware when this is happening, and perhaps give management impetus to it when you see new opportunities.

In Chapter 4 we shall consider how you can take a strategic look at the issues, and analyse how the systems in your organization and industry are evolving. Meanwhile, we can develop Figure 3.1 to the form shown in Figure 3.3.

We now have some dates and interrelationships shown. For most organizations the 1960s was the era of seeking savings and efficiency, the 1970s was the era of seeking effectiveness, and the 1980s was the time when they were

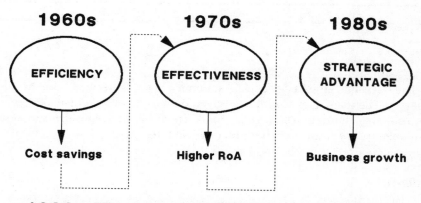

1990s: The integrated portfolio for IT/IS

Figure 3.3   *Generic benefits – 2*

exhorted to look for strategic advantage from IT/IS. As we have just seen, the categories are really not that simple. The 1990s will be about building an *integrated portfolio for IT/IS*, where as a manager you have deliberately weighed the generic benefits, perceive their interrelationship, and are clear how they all contribute to the benefit of the business.

Taking Stock

You should now be in a position to do the second part of the information management audit for your organization. This is shown in Figure 3.4.

Ser.	Question	Score	Action
Guideline: Distinguish the potential benefits of IT/IS			
1	Do you carefully consider all three generic benefits of IT/IS?		
2	Do you have some systems which seek mainly efficiency benefits?		
3	Can you identify those benefits, and the cost savings?		
4	Do you have some systems which seek mainly effectiveness benefits?		
5	Can you identify those benefits, and the increased return on assets?		
6	Do you have some systems which seek mainly strategic advantage (edge)?		
7	Can you identify those benefits, and the resulting business growth?		
8	Can you provide the right management framework for different benefits?		
9	Can you cope with differences between planned and actual benefits?		
10	Do you have an integrated portfolio for IT/IS?		
	TOTALS		

Figure 3.4   *IM audit – Part 2*

The questions, in effect, provide a summary of the issues addressed in this chapter. The method of scoring was given on page 6, and you will of course be ruthlessly honest, won't you? Think carefully, and consider the case examples which illustrate what other people have done.

References

Cobbin, W. F., Kozar, K. A. and Michaele, S. J. (1989), 'Establishing Telemarketing Leadership through Information Management', *MIS Quarterly*, Vol. 13, No. 3, pp. 360–72 (Sep.).

Galliers, R. D. (Ed) (1987), *Information Analysis: Selected Readings*, Addison-Wesley.

HMSO (1991), *Britain – An Official Handbook*, HMSO, London.

Kempner, T. (1987) (Ed.), *The Penguin Management Handbook*, 4th Edition, Penguin Books.

Malone, T.W., Yates, J. and Benjamin, R.I. (1989), 'The Logic of Electronic Markets', *Harvard Business Review*, Vol. 67, No. 3, pp. 166–70 (May–June).

Parkinson, L. K. and Parkinson, S. T. (1987), *Using the Microcomputer in Marketing*, McGraw-Hill.

Remenyi, D. S. J. (1990), *Strategic Information Systems: Development, Implementation, Case Studies*, NCC Blackwell.

4 How to think strategically

Introduction

As a senior manager you are concerned with the strategy of your business, or of a significant part of it. That sounds a reasonable proposition, but what exactly do we mean by 'senior manager' and 'strategy'?

In this chapter we first consider that question, to see what strategic thinking is all about, and how it differs from the normal tasks of management planning. We can then focus on some methods for strategic thinking, to help you follow our third guideline: 'Think strategically about information management'. This provides some conceptual tools against which to relate your own experience and the thirty examples mentioned in Chapter 3. The aim is for you to find out what is right and useful for *you*.

It becomes clear that information management is not something separate from other aspects of management. It should be an integral part of your thinking as a senior manager, receiving due attention alongside the others.

Senior managers and strategy

In Chapter 2 we used a simple definition of management:

MANAGERS direct RESOURCES to achieve RESULTS

Within the business organization it is usual to distinguish three levels of management. The junior, middle and senior managers are concerned respectively with the short-term (operational) planning and control, with medium-term planning, and with the long-term planning for the enterprise. Figure 4.1 shows an estimate by Constable and McCormick (1987) of the numbers of managers in the UK at each level.

From an employed workforce of 21.8 million people, about 2.75 million

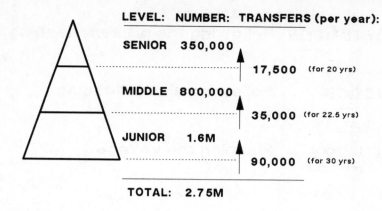

Figure 4.1   *UK management.* (Source: *Constable and McCormick, 1987*)

(12.6 per cent) exercised some management function. The figure also shows estimates of the number of people who moved into each level per year, and the expected time they would spend in that level.

This suggested that 1.6 per cent of the workforce were 'senior managers', but there was no clear definition of what that term meant. To distinguish the three levels of management more clearly, consider two related aspects of the work:

(a) The nature of management thinking.
(b) The time-horizon for management planning.

At junior level managers are concerned with the *operations* of the business. They look after day-to-day work, following existing policy, with clear precedents. They plan ahead only to the extent that this is necessary to support continued operations. For example, junior managers may arrange staff rosters, order raw materials, and plan the use of the facilities on a shop floor. Figure 4.2 uses a nautical analogy for the three levels; operational managers make sure the ship (the enterprise) continues to follow its present heading (direction) successfully.

At the middle level managers are concerned with the *tactics* of the business. They deal with changes to established operations, to respond to changed external factors or new policy received from senior levels. In the nautical analogy they guide the ship on to a new heading, by changing its immediate direction.

At senior level managers are concerned with *strategy* – the long-term

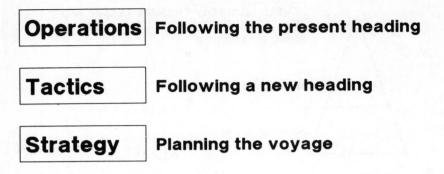

Figure 4.2   *Management levels*

direction of the business, perhaps to a goal which is not obvious at present. In the nautical analogy they plan the voyage. This requires thinking not just about a visible goal (whether fixed or changing), but about how to reach goals which are not yet visible though, they believe, appropriate and attainable. Thus strategic thinking is quite different from operational and tactical thinking. It is about creating the future, rather than reacting to the future.

What about the time-horizon of the associated management planning? Research by Jaques (1986) has shown that the time-horizon of planning is a better guide to the nature of management jobs than the job title or the age of the person doing the job. He found that in real organizations there are seven levels, such that people at one level consider people at the next level up to be their 'real managers'. What distinguishes the levels is the time-horizon of the planning which is done. Figure 4.3 shows Jaques' seven levels, the corresponding time-spans for planning, some representative names of posts in industry, and the cognitive states (or roles) at each level.

Jaques identifies Stratum V (with time-horizon 5–10 years) as a key transition zone. It represents the upper limit of forecasting the future based on the past – what we have called tactical management, or changing the heading. At Stratum V or above managers are *constructing* the future rather than *forecasting* it – what we have called strategic management, or planning the Voyage. Thus the 5-year planning time-span can be taken as the distinctive transition point to senior management.

The age at which an individual manager becomes equipped for such work varies from case to case. As we go through life our mental time-horizon expands, and ideally our job responsibilities should develop in step. It appears from the work of Jaques and others that the transition to a 5-year planning-horizon can occur roughly between age 28 (for those with potential for Stratum VII) and age 48 (for those whose comfortable ceiling is at Stratum V). It should be noted that the skills of people at these levels seem to go on

Stratum	Time-span	Industry post	Cognitive state
VII	20-50 yrs	Corporation head	Extrapolative devt of whole systems
VI	10-20 yrs	Group head	Definition of whole systems in world-wide envt
V	5-10 yrs	Subsidiary head	Shaping of whole systems from within
IV	2-5 yrs	General manager	Transformation of concrete systems
III	1-2 yrs	Unit head	Extrapolation in concrete systems
II	3 mths - 1 yr	Section head	Definition of tasks
I	1 day - 3 mths	Shop-floor worker	Shaping of concrete objects

Figure 4.3 *Cognitive states.* (Source: *Jaques, 1986*)

increasing even after normal retirement age. Perhaps that's reassuring, when considered from the viewpoint of the mature manager!

The skills needed for managers to operate effectively at this level have been surveyed and listed by Dulewicz (1989). Successful managers of high potential and of average age 40 were assessed by themselves and their bosses on forty specific management competences. Factor analysis of the results showed that there were twelve independent dimensions of performance, which can be termed 'supra-competences'. These are listed in Figure 4.4.

INTELLECTUAL	1. Strategic perspective
	2. Analysis and judgement
	3. Planning and organizing
INTERPERSONAL	4. Managing staff
	5. Persuasiveness
	6. Assertiveness and decisiveness
	7. Interpersonal sensitivity
	8. Oral communication
ADAPTABILITY	9. Adaptability and resilience
RESULTS-ORIENTATION	10. Energy and inititative
	11. Achievement-motivation
	12. Business sense

Figure 4.4 *Supra-competences.* (Source: *Dulewicz, 1989*)

'Strategic perspective' is one of the twelve; it includes the ability to rise above the detail to see broader issues (so-called 'helicopter vision'), and to take account of a wide range of influences both inside and outside the organization. These are among the key skills of senior managers.

We can say therefore:

- The distinctive role of senior managers is strategic management.
- This is about 'planning the voyage' for the enterprise, or a significant part of it, in a timescale of 5 years or more.
- It requires the ability to see the broader issues, both inside and outside the organization.
- A few individuals become mentally equipped for this by the time they are 30, but for most it will happen between age 38 and 48.

Strategic thinking

The ideas of strategy and tactics originated in a military context. The *Concise Oxford Dictionary* (1982) defines strategy as 'Generalship, the art of war ... management of an army or armies in a campaign, art of so moving or disposing troops or ships or aircraft as to impose upon the enemy the place and time and conditions for fighting preferred by oneself'. Professor Bernard Taylor of Henley Management College defines business strategy as 'Searching for the new rules of the game; then finding a way to win'.

It is interesting how the language of war is so often adopted now for the context of business. Managers speak of 'locking in customers', 'killing the competition' and 'fighting the battle'. We should be careful that the use of such language does not lead to a narrow-minded or vicious attitude to business. In recent years there has been, if anything, a swing towards acknowledging a wider responsibility; there are other stakeholders than the shareholders, and even the customer.

What's different about strategy? The essence of strategic thinking (planning the voyage) is shown in Figure 4.5.

There are three questions about the enterprise, shown at the top of the figure. The order of asking them is important:

1 *Where are we now?* We must take stock of the current business situation. This is often done with a strengths, weaknesses, opportunities and threats (SWOT) analysis. Strengths and weaknesses are mainly internal, and about present reality. Opportunities and threats are mainly external, and about the future prospect.
2 *Where do we want to be?* The answer to this question requires an act of lateral or intuitive thinking, to create a vision of where we want the

1. Where are we now?   **2. Where do we want to be?**

3. How will we get there?

Figure 4.5   *Strategy*

enterprise to be in several years' time. It may be very different from what it is like now, or even from what lies along the current heading. The vision defines the destination of the voyage.

3   *How will we get there?* This plans the voyage itself, and defines the critical success factors (CSFs) which must be achieved if the whole voyage is to be successful. The CSFs can be considered as marker buoys or other features along the route of the voyage.

The relation between the three questions is shown in the middle part of Figure 4.5. The SWOT represents the assessment of the current situation, in some detail. The dotted line shows the creative and visionary act. I have been privileged to watch this creative thinking happen in groups of managers during practical workshops on business strategy. It is a fascinating process when a close team, by now fully immersed in the situation of the enterprise they are considering, begin to formulate the possible 'futures' for that enterprise, and choose the *vision* which is a challenging yet attainable goal making business sense. In terms of time this creative act and discussion may be quite quick compared with the preceding and subsequent work on the detail. Yet it is of unrivalled importance in terms of leading the organization into the future. It is the creative mental act which sets the senior manager, and the leader, apart. He or she creates the vision, communicates it and then leads others towards it.

The *strategy* is the broad plan for the route of the voyage to the vision. It might, for example, include intentions to diversify the product range, extend the geographical coverage of operations, grow through merger or acquisition, use modern technology to fuller effect, or other such broad management intentions.

The lower part of Figure 4.5 shows the next level of detail below the 'SWOT, Vision and Strategy'. At this lower level items should be specific, quantified and timed. Thus *objectives* are the specific interpretation of the vision. They might include:

(a) To be UK market-leader in the sale of mid-range widgets by 1996.
(b) To achieve 30 per cent market share for each of our products within 3 years.
(c) To reduce the cost of a public-sector service by 15 per cent in real terms within 4 years.

Critical success factors (CSFs) are markers along that route: points which must be reached and passed if the strategy is to be successful. The CSFs should be expressed in quantified terms (say turnover, profit, or market share at a certain date), so that they are objective measures and there will be no doubt or argument as to whether they have been achieved or not.

Performance indicators (PIs) are management measures which can be used to check progress along each part of the voyage: from one CSF to the next. CSFs might be spaced a year or more apart in time; PIs check progress at the tactical level within a shorter timescale. PIs might monitor the same quantities, such as market share, as are used to define the CSFs. But they might monitor related quantities, e.g. a reduction in the number of employees as one step towards reducing the cost of a public-sector operation.

The terminology suggested here is consistent and useful, but by no means unique. Often the first step in a strategy discussion is for the participants to agree the meaning of terms such as 'strategy' and 'objectives'! However, a top-down approach, based on the three critical questions asked in the right order, is an essential feature of strategic thinking.

The IM challenge

Strategic thinking requires you to take the wider view – both inside, and more especially outside, the enterprise. You need to be conscious of the political, social and business environment in which are seeking to survive and grow. There is no shortage of challenges at this level. Figure 4.6 lists a dozen of them.

Each of those twelve issues could cause sleepless nights, and long debates about corporate policy. One of the problems in thinking widely about the environment is to draw a line between that which we need to consider, and can perhaps influence, and that over which we have little influence and must

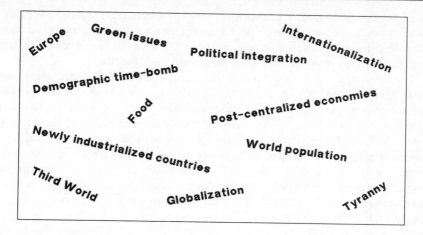

Figure 4.6   *Challenge – 1*

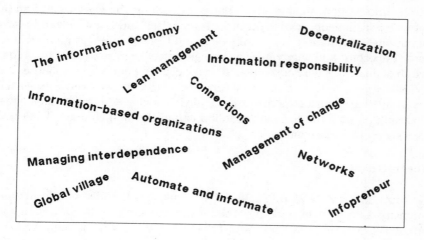

Figure 4.7   *Challenge – 2*

therefore accept. There is a wise prayer which asks for serenity to accept what we cannot change, courage to change what we can, and wisdom to know the difference.

Figure 4.7 lists a further set of challenging issues, closer to the area of information management.

Let's look at what lies behind some of the words shown. The phrase 'automate and informate' comes from Zuboff (1988). She has coined the word 'informate' to contrast with the familiar word 'automate'. To automate is to reinforce the command-and-control style of management, based on organizational and functional hierarchy. To informate is to enable work to be done more flexibly, with a higher level of personal responsibility. It is about enabling and facilitating, rather than about specifying and directing.

This idea, and some of the other words in Figure 4.7, accord with the views of Drucker (1988) about the future role of people in 'information-based organizations'. He uses analogies such as the symphony orchestra and the hospital to illustrate how people take individual responsibility, while working towards a collective goal. To do this they must 'take information responsibility' – be concerned with the purposeful use of information as a resource. Another commentator, Rockart (1988), has emphasized that this will not remain the preserve of senior managers only, but increasingly devolve to lower levels of management also; it must be part of the corporate culture. At a more prosaic level the 'information economy' reflects the ever-growing importance of the service sector of the economy, which we saw in Chapter 2. Some people see IT/IS as an enabler, to make it possible for the organization to respond to the changing environment.

The information management challenge is about these issues and many more. It is a challenge both to the organization itself and to the wider economy of nations. Information as a commodity, and IT/IS as an investment, will be more important and will require a strategic response by management. What we shall do next is look at some methods of deciding upon that response. We take three perspectives: the internal view (focusing on the enterprise itself), the external view (focusing on the external environment) and the dynamic view (focusing on how the strategic situation can evolve and change). The three views are of course complementary.

The internal view

First, the internal view. In Chapter 2 we looked at the idea of information intensity as a way of deciding whether 'information' is important in the product or in the process. Porter *et al.* (1985) used the idea of the value chain to develop the process aspect, and this is shown in Figure 4.8.

It represents, diagramatically, the various activities within the organization which collectively make up the process of production. The 'primary' activities are directly related to the production of the good or the service. They are illustrated in the context of a manufacturing operation, with inbound materials, a production process, outbound goods and product sales and support. The 'secondary' activities relate to the infrastructure of the operation: both tangible (e.g. buildings and offices) and intangible (e.g. administrative costs). The total cost of all these activities makes up the total cost of the process. It should be lower than the market value of the goods or services produced, and the difference represents the margin. Figure 4.8 is merely a diagrammatic

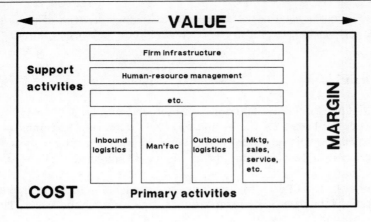

Figure 4.8 *Value chain. (Derived from Porter and Millar, 1985)*

representation of the profit and loss account, but can help you to focus on information intensity within the process. Where information is important, there may be scope for getting benefit from IT/IS.

You should be able to identify opportunities in most of the cost-areas of the value chain. For example, in a specialist small-order light engineering company *primary-activity* opportunities might include:

(a) *Inbound logistics*: electronic data interchange (EDI) links with suppliers; integrated production, stock-control and materials resource planning (MRP) systems.
(b) *Manufacturing*: computer numerically controlled (CNC) machine-tools; electronic linking of computer-aided design (CAD) systems to production systems.
(c) *Outbound logistics*: EDI links with customers; customized labelling and packing; links with order processing and invoicing systems, to improve billing and cash-flow.
(d) *Marketing, sales, and service*: closer links with customers (for this business, the customer might play an active part in the CAD work, for example); computer-assisted response to service enquiries.

Support-activity opportunities might include:

(a) *Infrastructure*: energy-saving measures; improved building management; vehicle-fleet management and route/loading optimization.
(b) *HRM*: personnel management systems; matching of individual skills with job needs, both long- and short-term.

The value-chain is like most of the other conceptual tools: a set of ideas, or an agenda, for you to interpret in the context of your own organization.

The external view

The value chain is mainly about internal improvements, for better efficiency or effectiveness. It is clear, though, that external interfaces with suppliers and customers are important aspects of the value chain. They are one aspect of the broader, external view of the enterprise which as a senior manager you need to take.

Figure 4.9 shows Porter's classic five-force model of industry competitiveness, and lists the three generic business strategies (Porter and Millar, 1985).

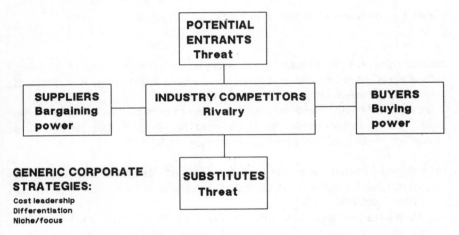

Figure 4.9   *Competitive forces. (Source: Porter and Millar, 1985)*

The model is useful to judge the current situation, the opportunities and the threats in your industry. For example:

- A wholesale clothing manufacturer, such as S R Gent in Chapter 3, might consider overseas competitors, and a powerful single customer, to be the major external factors. The threats from cloth-suppliers, new entrants to the UK scene, and from substitutes (are there any?) would probably be less.
- A retail bank will certainly worry about new entrants (other financial institutions, in a liberalized market), and customers. They will worry about their industry competitors (other retail banks), depending on their current position in the pecking order.

- A public body like the police has no immediate industry competitors, but there are new entrants and substitutes for various aspects of security and protection. They will have deep concern about suppliers of resources (mainly local authorities in the UK) and customers (the public, both individually and collectively).

This overview of the industry situation is necessary to decide where your strategic priorities lie. It is too simple to say that the aim of business is to satisfy (or even to delight) the customer. That is true for most organizations in the long term, but in the short term there may be more pressing matters of competition or new entrants. If you operate cross-Channel ferries your thinking will be dominated by the Channel Tunnel. You may be unable to compete on cost, and may have to differentiate your product in other ways if you are to survive.

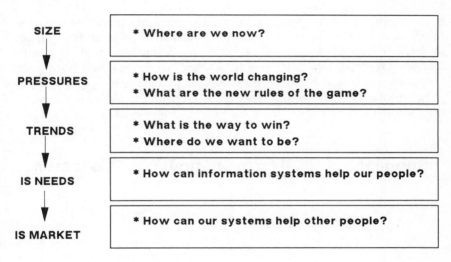

Figure 4.10   *Sector analysis*

Let's move on to an agenda to develop this external view of your business further. It is called sector analysis, and is shown in Figure 4.10, where an agenda of questions focusses on the future changes (threats and opportunities) for your enterprise. The questions concern:

1 *Size.* The current situation, in terms of a SWOT and competitive forces analysis.
2 *Pressures.* The external pressures on the industry in which you operate. The pressures may come from a change in competitive forces (a new

entrant perhaps) or in the regulatory environment (by government changing the rules), or by a change in the attitude of your customers or society at large (fashion, concern for 'green' issues, for example).

3   *Trends.* What changes will these pressures induce that will affect your business (lower profit margins, more direct competition, lower demand for your traditional product, rejection of certain materials, e.g. fur).

4   *IS needs.* What needs and opportunity for IT/IS arise in the new business situation? Can IT/IS enable you to win by being quicker to respond to the new situation, by differentiating your product, by making your business process more efficient?

5   *IS market.* Do the changes result in a business opportunity for you to sell 'information' or special IT/IS into a wider market? Remember this was the fourth suggested way of gaining strategic advantage discussed in Chapter 3.

Some illustrations of this analysis, in various sectors of industry, are given in Knight and Silk (1990). Conceptually the sequence of questions fits with our model of strategic thinking (Figure 4.5); the creative business thinking is in the analysis of the trends, deciding how the business can win in the changed world out there, and how it needs to equip itself for that change.

The third and final idea in this section is illustrated in Figure 4.11, which shows how the firm's value chain fits into the wider world.

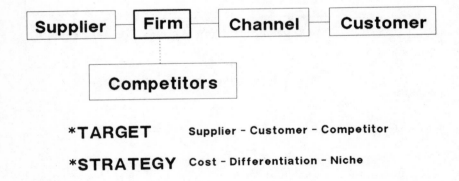

Figure 4.11   *External value chain*

The figure is a synthesis of the general ideas of industry competitiveness and generic strategy. It shows the firm's relationship with its suppliers, customers, and competitors. The 'channel' through which customers are reached may be a third-party business (such as a retailer) or it may be part of the firm's own operation (such as a dedicated logistics network). The channel can be very important in the industry power-balance, and can have scope for using IT/IS to augment or replace traditional channels:

(a) For retail banks, ATM machines replace a face-to-face channel across a counter.
(b) For home banking, telephone lines replace both human tellers and ATMs for information exchange between the customer and the bank, but not for cash-dispensing.
(c) For the distribution of high-value products, courier services can replace the traditional channels of post or the firm's own delivery service.

Use Figure 4.11 to consider:

(i) Where the threats and opportunities lie for your business.
(ii) Which part your strategy should target.
(iii) Which generic business strategy you will use.
(iv) Where you can use IT/IS to good effect to support that strategy.

The dynamic view

So far in this chapter we have:

- Identified the distinctive task for senior managers of strategic thinking (the holistic view, with the 5-year planning-horizon).
- Defined the essential characteristics of strategic thinking (the three-part process depicted in Figure 4.5).
- Reviewed the broad challenge to managers, at a general level and in respect of information management.
- Looked at some aids to strategic thinking, first from the internal and then the external perspective.

This might be sufficient if the world stood still, but it doesn't! Throughout the 1980s and into the 1990s the pace of business change has been accelerating. As managers, should we just respond to this as it comes, or try to see ahead?

There can be only one answer to that question: we must develop our thinking not just about a *new* future but about a *changing* future. Our third view of strategic information management is therefore about the dynamics of change.

We have already mentioned and used two simple ideas: the three generic benefits of IT/IS, and the three levels of management in the organization. Let's bring these ideas together into a management 'map', called the benefit-level matrix (BLM), as shown in Figure 4.12.

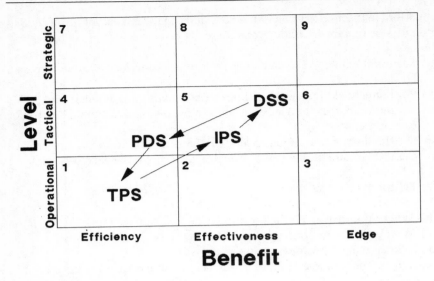

Figure 4.12   *Benefit-level matrix – 1*

The BLM is used to plot the characteristics of information systems, according to the type of benefit they give, and the level of management to which they bring that benefit:

(a) The horizontal X-axis in Figure 4.12 shows the three generic benefits (efficiency, effectiveness, and strategic advantage or competitive edge). We saw from the practical examples in Chapter 3 that the generic benefit is determined not only by the technology of the system itself but also by the management intention and context within which it is used. Taking these together, we can usually define the main generic benefit in a particular case.

(b) The vertical Y-axis shows the three levels of the organization (operational, tactical, and strategic). An information system is plotted to show which level of management gets the benefit. It is important to realize that this may *not* be the same level as the managers who planned and approved the system. Rather, it is the level at which its subsequent impact is felt.

These axes define nine boxes or cells in the BLM, which have been numbered 1–9 for convenience. This gives enough categories to plot the evolution of systems as their business context changes.

Figure 4.12 gives a fairly common example of this. We shall explain the acronyms as we go along, although they are in widespread use now. The sequence shown is as follows:

1   A transaction processing system (TPS) was introduced to deal with day-to-day operations in a particular area of the business. It might have been a stock-control system in a manufacturing company, or a mainframe system introduced in the 1960s mainly for efficiency benefits (to save people). The TPS is shown in Cell 1 because its impact is at the operational level, and its main benefit is efficiency.

2   After the TPS had been operating for about a year, it was realized that it held a mass of detailed data which, if suitably summarized, would provide useful management information in the form of routine or exception reports. An information provision system (IPS) performs this role. It might have been added to the original TPS, but would more commonly be an integral feature of any modern TPS. In our example the IPS might provide monthly consumption figures for the various items of stock; this would be information which middle-level managers would use in making their purchasing and replenishment decisions. The IPS should be able to produce the information they require, in the format best suited to their needs. It should therefore make the middle managers more effective in their decision-making. Cell 5 is therefore appropriate.

3   In the light of the improved information the stock managers realized they could be more subtle in their decision-making. As PCs became more powerful, they found they had the tools to explore other options. The essential feature of such decision support systems (DSS) is that they contain a model of the system being managed, with which the manager can experiment. The DSS enables him to get a feel for the problem, and explore various options in quantified detail, before reaching a final decision. Many longstanding statistical and operational research (OR) techniques have now become practical, with the cheap and convenient power of modern computers.

4   Eventually the decision-making process about stock replenishment became well understood, and optimized for the needs of the stock-control operation. There was then no need for middle managers to take the routine decisions: the data could be fed directly to the modelling system, and, with the decision criteria defined, the system could make the routine decisions itself. The results would then be passed to operational level for implementation. Not so many middle managers were needed, so savings could be made. The PDS was thus an efficiency system, in Cell 4.

5   It then became clear that the decisions could be passed, in the form of replenishment orders, to the TPS in electronic form. Routine decisions could then be made and implemented without intervention. The whole operation therefore became a routine operational matter, in Cell 1.

This example illustrates several important points about the evolution of IT/IS. A system often starts at the operational level; its impact then becomes felt further up the organization; improved business procedures can then be developed and automated; and the whole operation becomes a routine feature at the operational level (though more complex than before). Cell 1 represents 'business as usual', but is evolving in step with the development of the company. If this is successful and becomes known outside, others will imitate it. Cell 1 will then represent an 'industry norm' that is continually evolving.

How long does it all take? The answer will vary with each case, but for a large organization following the sequence described it might take 5–10 years. More often than not, in real organizations, this progression takes place piecemeal. The value of the BLM is that you can see what you are doing on a conceptual 'map' and thereby plan ahead.

Figure 4.13 adds some further examples of the evolution and migration of IT/IS on the BLM.

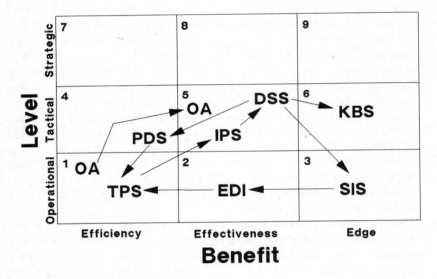

Figure 4.13   *Benefit-level matrix – 2*

The first addition is office automation (OA). For many organizations OA was first used, in the form of standalone word processors, as a productivity aid for typists in the typing pool. This belongs in Cell 1, Figure 4.13. Later the technology of local area networks (LANs) allowed terminals to be linked together, and they had other uses than just word processing. OA became a processing, storage and communication facility throughout the organization. At middle levels it brought effectiveness benefits: accountants were better at their job because they had spreadsheet and financial modelling resources; and marketing staff became more effective because they could control their resources and build models for product-mix and the marketing plan. This aspect of OA therefore becomes evident in Cell 5.

Knowledge-based systems (KBS), usually in the form of expert systems, were often a development of DSS. The best available expertise would be captured in the KBS and used to full effect. An example of this was Blue Circle Cement, discussed on pages 13–14 and page 30. For BCC, this was an edge system bringing competitive advantage, and is shown in Cell 6.

So far, strategic or edge systems have usually been innovations at the operational level (although conceived and planned at a higher level). Thus the American Airlines reservation system SABRE and the Thomson Holidays TOPS systems would be in Cell 3 when they were introduced. Although they were strategic information systems (SIS) in terms of their benefit, they were at the operational level in terms of their immediate impact. They gave their owners a real competitive edge. Gradually, though, all good things come to an end: electronic links with customers were imitated, and became the industry norm. In the form of electronic data interchange (EDI) they even became subject to standardization: for example, TRADANET for UK food retailing, and EDIFACT for international EDI standards.

This presents a dilemma for companies at the leading edge: should they participate in emerging industry standards, or should they develop or retain their own distinctive systems? By remaining separate there is opportunity to lock-in customers or suppliers with a specialist system which can be developed to mutual advantage. On the other hand, those customers and suppliers might opt for industry standards which they see as giving them wider choice. It all depends on how big you are, and the balance of power. There are examples of Ford opting out of the automotive industry EDI system, and of BHS (a major retailer) opting out of the TRADANET system, no doubt for carefully considered business reasons.

For a while EDI might give a benefit of effectiveness (Cell 2), but as it becomes the industry norm, it migrates to Cell 1 (business as usual). This migration from Cell 3 to Cell 1 has taken perhaps 5 years in the examples mentioned.

A few key points about the BLM so far:

1   It is a convenient way of understanding the evolution of systems related to business initiatives and to the emerging industry standards.
2   It offers a method for consciously planning ahead.
3   Competitive advantage (edge) is ephemeral; you need to recognize this and plan your 'encore' if you are to sustain the competitive advantage.

Why has nothing been shown so far at the strategic level (Cells 7–9) of the BLM? Well, there is less to report there, and perhaps a greater opportunity. Figure 4.14 shows some possibilities.

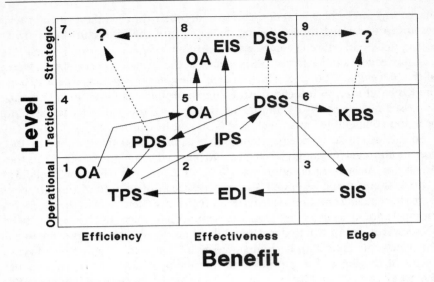

Figure 4.14   *Benefit-level matrix – 3*

Cell 8 certainly has current examples. Office automation (OA) has penetrated to senior levels; indeed the success of office networks often depends on the support and actions of senior management. Executive information systems (EIS) are extensions of information provision systems (IPS) used further down the organization. The key features of EIS are that they not only give a simple overview of the performance of the business, in a format chosen and evolved by senior managers, but they also allow the user to 'drill down' into the underlying data to explore in more detail the reasons for any aspect of the presentation. EIS are usually integrated into a decision-making environment tailored to the needs of senior management teams. As part of this, they may use decision support systems (DSS), which have become more complex and deal with a wider range of aspects of the business than the more specialist versions used at middle-management level. All these examples in Cell 8 can be tools of effectiveness at senior level, and their use is developing quite rapidly.

This still leaves question marks about Cells 7 and 9 in Figure 4.14. Is it that efficiency and edge benefits at the strategic level are simply not possible? This is an issue for your careful consideration, as a senior manager operating at that level. Could it be that just as operational-level staff were squeezed and trimmed by the first wave of application of IT/IS in business, and middle management by the second, that senior management's turn has now come as well?

There are a few leading-edge examples which might fit into Cell 9. They are knowledge-based systems which encapsulate case-histories of business strategy, and guide the senior manager on the basis of success in similar situations elsewhere. Gongla *et al.* (1989) describe such a system operating at the level of business strategy, and Ho (1991) has developed a similar system for small and medium enterprises (SMEs) in the manufacturing and service sectors.

To summarize, the benefit-level matrix (BLM) is in a format familiar to general managers. The axes relate easily to the structure of the business and to the generic benefits which IT/IS can offer. The nine cells of the matrix offer fine enough detail to plot the historical development of IT/IS. This highlights both the dynamic nature of the use of IT (and the ephemeral nature of competitive advantage), and directs your attention to areas which have not yet been fully exploited. It therefore has useful advantages as a framework for management thinking.

The information strategy

In this chapter we have introduced some aids to strategic thinking which have been found useful in practice. There are many others to choose from: see, for example, Ward (1990). There is some evidence that the precise tool used is less important than the commitment and motivation of those who are using it. My experience is that the tools described here will provide a 'spark' for most people.

It is no good thinking strategically unless those thoughts are captured, and then applied to the benefit of the enterprise. We have seen how thinking about the business and thinking about 'information' must go hand in hand. That thinking should lead to a business strategy and a related information strategy. Of course you may well need strategy documents for other facets of management, such as human-resource management (HRM). These are not our primary concern here, although there may well be links with the information strategy.

Have *you* got an information strategy which is part of, or closely linked to, the business strategy? Surveys show that things are improving: 60–70 per cent of UK companies now do. So what is an information strategy? Figure 4.15 shows the main features.

The information strategy should be recorded formally in a document. Being strategic, it should take the long-term view – usually a 5-year view, which is often as far as one can see in a world where both the business situation and the technology are changing so rapidly. The information strategy should therefore be reviewed perhaps annually or every 18 months. This should be done in detail by the senior IT/IS steering committee, which is usually chaired by a senior general manager (see page 21). It should then be considered and approved by the top-level management team: the board or its equivalent.

The information strategy provides the framework for the development and

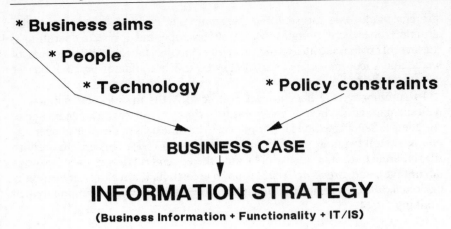

Figure 4.15   *Information strategy*

use of IT/IS in the enterprise to support business aims. The left-hand side of Figure 4.15 shows how the logic of the argument should proceed:

1   What are the business aims, and what is the place of 'information' as a resource in achieving those aims?
2   How do people actually need to work in order to achieve those aims? In particular, what information do they require, and how do they need to process and communicate that information?
3   How can the technology (IT/IS) be used to collect, process, store and communicate that information?

There is an important point to stress here. It doesn't matter where the bright ideas start from, but this logical sequence must be able to support the resulting decisions. Thus an IT professional may point out a new piece of technology which might be of value. His general manager colleagues may then discuss this in a business context, consult the people who would use it, and then decide that it would indeed benefit the business. This process requires the effective information management partnership which we discussed in Chapter 2. In the information strategy document the argument does not follow the way the idea grew chronologically; rather it is based upon the logical sequence which starts with business aims.

The right-hand side of Figure 4.15 shows 'policy constraints'. These are factors which must be taken into account as part of the management thinking. They often limit freedom of action, but they are sometimes decisions about the future. Examples of policy constraints are:

(a) Investment in existing IT/IS is substantial. New systems must interface with these existing systems, at least for the duration of their remaining economic life.
(b) The company feels uncomfortably 'locked-in' to one particular vendor of IT/IS. To correct this, the information strategy might specify that future systems should have industry standards rather than proprietary standards. This will give a wider choice in future development. The emerging standards for open systems interconnection (OSI) are an important general opportunity here; most major vendors recognize that it is in their interests, as well as the interests of their customers, to support these standards. There are other standards, or developments of OSI, for special areas; examples are EDIFACT for electronic data interchange (EDI), and manufacturing automation protocol (MAP) and total office protocol (TOP) for production and office systems.
(c) An actual or potential merger/acquisition requires hitherto separate information systems to be brought together to support the new pattern of business. This can be difficult; there are examples of mergers which have failed because of IT/IS incompatibility, and mergers which have been given a good impetus because the integration of IT/IS was well-planned and fairly straightforward.

The two threads come together in Figure 4.15 to give the business case for the information strategy, which may be at a quite general level: identifying the generic benefits in as much detail as possible. For efficiency benefits there should be an estimate of cost savings; for effectiveness benefits there should be an explanation of the improved RoA of other resources; and for edge benefits there should be an explanation of how the business will grow, or margins/profit be improved. Chapter 5 will discuss the business case for individual systems in more detail.

The product of all this is the core of the information strategy: the framework for use of IT/IS to support the enterprise. It might be at three levels, which reflect the three stages in the supporting logical argument:

1 A 'business information' strategy, saying how information will be used to support the business.
2 An 'IS functionality' strategy, saying what functionality (features and performance) people need from the information systems.
3 An 'IT/IS' strategy which defines the policy for hardware and software. It will include issues like the hardware and software architecture, standards, preferred suppliers, and preferred ranges of products/services.

In a small or simple business one information strategy might be enough. In a conglomerate of several contrasting products or businesses there will usually be several. The trend is to have a 'minimalist' corporate information strategy, and give maximum freedom within that to the individual strategic business units (SBUs). This organizational aspect relates to our discussion on pages 18–21. A corporate information strategy would often deal with:

(a) Corporate-level information needs, such as the type and format of financial reporting to the centre.
(b) Common system architectures, to make best use of in-house expertise, and establish effective relationships with vendors.
(c) Organizational arrangements to ensure SBU strategies accord with (and possibly help develop) the corporate strategy.

Taking stock

The whole of this chapter has been about taking the strategic view, in a changing world. We have defined what this means, and described some aids to strategic thinking. The 'information' aspect is often very important. The result needs to be captured in the information strategy, as a basis for further and more detailed work.

Before we go on and think about individual systems in more detail, you need to take stock of the practice in YOUR enterprise. You should by now be familiar with this searching, and sometimes painful, procedure. If you need a reminder about the marking procedure it is on page 6. The questions for Part 3 of the Information Management Audit are given in Figure 4.16.

Guideline: Think strategically about information management			
Ser.	Question	Score	Action
1	Do you have senior managers using strategic cognitive skills?		
2	Do you use the three-step creative approach to vision and strategy?		
3	Do you recognize the information aspect of the challenge to managers?		
4	Have you considered the internal view of strategy enough?		
5	Have you considered the external view of strategy enough?		
6	Have you considered the dynamic view of strategy enough?		
7	Can you use the benefit-level matrix to plot the evolution of your IT/IS?		
8	Can you use the BLM to plan ahead, for the industry and your enterprise?		
9	Do you have an information strategy closely linked to business strategy?		
10	Does the information strategy cover business, functionality, and IT/IS?		
	TOTALS		

Figure 4.16   *IM audit – Part 3*

You should recognize the issues which lie behind the set of ten questions; they provide an *aide-memoire* of the issues addressed in this chapter. You may want to look back over what we have covered, to help you answer accurately. Good luck!

References

Constable J. and McCormick, R. (1987), *The Making of British Managers*, British Institute of Management/Confederation of British Industry (BIM/CBI), April.

Drucker, P. F. (1988), 'The Coming of the New Organization', *Harvard Business Review*, Vol. 66, No. 1, pp. 45–53 (Jan.–Feb.).

Dulewicz, S. V. (1989), 'Assessment Centres as the Route to Competence', *Personnel Management* (Nov.).

Gongla, P. *et al.* (1989), 'S*P*A*R*K: A Knowledge-Based System for Identifying Competitive Uses of Information Technology', *IBM Systems Journal*, Vol. 28, No. 4, pp. 628–45 (Dec.).

Ho, S. (1991), 'Effective Applications of Microcomputer-Based Management Information and Decision Support Systems for Small and Medium Enterprises', PhD Dissertation, Brunel University (April).

Jaques, E. (1986), 'The Development of Intellectual Capability: a Discussion of Stratified Systems Theory', *Journal of Applied Behavioral Science*, Vol. 22, No. 4, pp. 361–83.

Knight, A. V. and Silk, D. J. (1990), *Managing Information*, McGraw-Hill, London.

Porter, M. E. and Millar, V. E. (1985), 'How Information gives you Competitive Advantage', *Harvard Business Review*, Vol. 63, No. 4, pp. 149–60 (July–Aug.).

Rockart, J. F. (1988), 'The Line takes the Leadership – IS Management in a Wired Society', *Sloan Management Review*, Vol. 29, No. 4, pp. 57–64 (Summer).

Ward, J. M. (1990), *Strategic IS Planning*, Wiley.

Zuboff, S. (1988), *In the Age of the Smart Machine*, Heinemann, London.

5 Identifying the benefits, and their value

Introduction

Much management thinking and discussion follows a two-stage sequence. First there is a broadening of the scope of the discussion, to consider the many related issues and see them in context. This is followed by a narrowing of the scope of the discussion, to reach a decision and to initiate action. They can be called the 'diverge' and 'converge' stages of the discussion, often corresponding to the definition and the resolution of a management problem. In a meeting it is important that the participants share a common view as to which stage they are in, particularly if time is pressing. If you are chair of the meeting, then you need to be careful how you lead it from the diverge to the converge stage. A good way to do so is to sum up the first stage, identify the main issues, and then lead into the second stage. This has been called 'putting a peg in the ground': summarizing what has been agreed, so that it is not subsequently re-examined and can be used as the basis for the second stage of the debate. Think about this in the context of meetings you have known. Commonly the transition is not achieved smoothly, and not enough time is left for the converge stage. Converging takes time, especially if you are trying to achieve consensus.

This book follows the same sequence. In the first half we progressively broadened our thinking about information management, until in Chapter 4 its relation with the widest aspects of business strategy became apparent. The information strategy is the 'peg in the ground' used by senior management to capture that part of the process. In this chapter we start to converge – to consider the more detailed aspects of Information Management concerned with the justification, implementation and successful operation of systems.

Sharpening the business case

We mentioned the 'business case' as a step in the logical justification of the information strategy. In that regard we have identified so far:

- The three generic benefits of IT/IS: efficiency, effectiveness, and strategic advantage or edge.
- The broad measures by which those benefits can be measured: cost, return on assets, and profit/growth.

This categorization is shown in the top part of Figure 5.1.

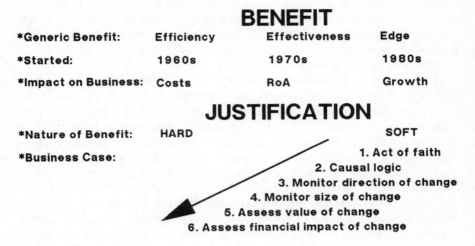

BENEFIT

*Generic Benefit:	Efficiency	Effectiveness	Edge
*Started:	1960s	1970s	1980s
*Impact on Business:	Costs	RoA	Growth

JUSTIFICATION

*Nature of Benefit: HARD   SOFT

*Business Case:
1. Act of faith
2. Causal logic
3. Monitor direction of change
4. Monitor size of change
5. Assess value of change
6. Assess financial impact of change

Figure 5.1 *The business case*

It is a broad but useful classification, and is supported by systematic research, e.g. by Weill and Olson (1989). The problem of course is that as the emphasis has shifted from pure efficiency systems to systems which incorporate the full range of generic benefits, then it has become more difficult to put financial figures on those benefits. The benefits have moved from 'hard' to 'soft', and they have therefore become more difficult to quantify. Organizations can respond to this difficulty in two ways:

1 They may *insist* upon a quantified financial justification as part of the business case for a proposed system, even though the main benefits may not be the saving of costs. This leads to a succession of best guesses to interpret 'soft' benefits in 'hard' terms. The confidence in the resulting figures must therefore be low, but the figures are required by the justification procedure which has been found appropriate in the past.
2 They may bypass the established procedures, and senior managers can approve projects on a much more subjective basis. They recognize that quantifying all the benefits is unrealistic, but they have no methodical alternative. They therefore approve the project as an intuitive act of faith.

This polarization often happens. Systems proposed at the middle or lower levels of the organization are bound by one set of rules; those originating at senior level (often strategic) are subject to different, and less clearly defined, sets of rules (or to no known rules at all!). A minority (often including accountants) will sometimes claim that if you think long and hard enough about benefits, they can always be expressed in financial terms. Most managers, however, do not share this view.

This polarization of practice is not satisfactory. We need a method for dealing with both hard and soft benefits. We need deliberately to try to sharpen up the business case, whilst recognizing that this will not be completely achieved in all cases. Let's identify some milestones in this process of sharpening up the business case.

First, we need to consider a special case: so-called 'must-do' projects – projects, or more usually developments of an existing system, which the enterprise simply has to do if it is to remain in business. There is no practical alternative. An example might be a change in the format in which the tax authorities require the company to render returns. Thus the change must be done in order to comply with new legal requirements, new regulations, or overwhelming pressure from suppliers or customers. An example of the last is the way that a major motor manufacturer or supermarket will require all its suppliers to use EDI for the ordering and accounting interface. If you are a supplier and you don't comply, then you simply lose that business. For some suppliers this would be business suicide. If you are faced with a 'must-do' requirement, then there is not much point in spending a lot of effort on assembling a business case. It is better to grin (if you can) and get on with it.

It is important to recognize the 'must-do' category, but in addition to that special case, we can identify six milestones in sharpening up the business case. These are shown in the lower part of Figure 5.1.

The first is the *Act of faith*. It is the extreme form of an intuitive judgement, which simply believes that the proposed system is right for the business. It may be that a senior manager has become seized with a particular idea, or that the benefits are so intangible or high-risk that it is not possible to assemble a conventional business case. Either way, senior management makes the decision and takes the responsibility for it.

Slightly better is the *Causal logic* type of argument. Here the cause-and-effect chain is identified, linking the provision of the information system with the resulting business benefit. Thus the reason for the business benefit is identified, although not the size of it.

The next stage is to *Monitor direction of change*. This extends the causal-logic case by defining some observable quantity which, after implementation of the system, can be measured in order to check that the business has indeed moved in the intended beneficial direction.

Better still is to *Monitor size of change*. In this case the size of the change in the observable quantity is estimated beforehand, and this change is checked quantitatively when the system is in operation.

The next milestone is to *Assess value of change*, giving the observable quantities some considered weighting so that different types of benefit can be compared with each other.

The final stage is to *Assess financial impact of change*, by giving each of the benefits a financial value. Not only can they then be compared with each other in money terms, but the impact on business performance measures can be calculated.

These six milestones enable you to sharpen up the business case to the extent that the 'hardness' or 'softness' of the benefits makes appropriate. They provide an alternative to the polarized situation which has so often arisen in the past. On pages 72–78 we shall consider some practical examples, and apply these milestones to the business case for two different types of information system.

The business case: current practice

First, though, let's look at current practice in this area. We have already mentioned the polarization between the act of faith and the 'hard' financial case. Figure 5.2 shows the results of asking a large group of managers about what actually happens in their organizations.

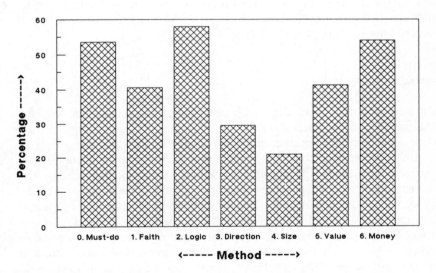

Figure 5.2 *IS justification. (Source: 281 managers at Henley, 1990)*

The source of the data was 281 managers passing through general-management courses at Henley (UK) in the period January to November 1990. They were successful managers of average age 40. Horizontally, the seven bars of the chart relate to the 'must-do' category, and then to the six milestones just identified. The seven categories were explained to the managers, and then in group discussion they identified which of the methods of making the business case were actually used in their organizations. The average *number* of methods identified for each organization was nearly three (out of seven). The vertical axis shows the percentage of managers identifying each of the seven methods.

We can draw the following tentative conclusions from this survey:

(a) The must-do category is important, being recognized by over 50 per cent of the organizations represented.
(b) For the remaining six methods (milestones), there is a general polarization of practice between 'soft' and 'hard' methods.
(c) At the 'soft' end 'Faith' seems to be giving way to the slightly more demanding discipline of a 'Logic' justification.
(d) In the middle ground there seems to be considerable scope for using the milestones for sharpening up the business case by identifying (and if possible quantifying) the changes in observable parameters.
(e) At the 'hard' end it seems accepted that value judgement is necessary, because not all benefits can be expressed in financial terms.

This survey of current practice should be a useful yardstick against which you can judge the practice in your own organization. In particular it may identify whether you have a polarization of practice at the moment, and could therefore improve things in the future.

Example: retail system

We'll now illustrate these ideas with practical example, and see how the business case can be sharpened up.

Consider a retail supermarket that sells mainly food. It is mid-range in price and quality of products sold. The competition in this sector is quite intense; there are competitors (who are also household names) located nearby. The management is keen to gain some competitive edge, but has already taken the obvious steps. The supermarket has modern point of sale (POS) systems, linked into stock-control and ordering systems with electronic data interchange (EDI) with all their main suppliers. More recently it has introduced electronic price tagging, so that the price displayed on the shelf beside a stock of items can be changed electronically; the current price is held in memory and is used by the POS system when items are checked out with the bar-code reader.

Thus it seems to be well up with industry standards, but perhaps IT can help it further?

Wisely, the senior managers had each been reading a copy of this book. While reading Chapter 4 they had begun to think about possible methods of gaining competitive edge. The marketing director was quite keen to understand his customers better, while the purchasing manager was keen to make better use of the short-term fluctuations in price in some of the wholesale markets he used for fresh produce. As a result of prodding by these two, the senior management team had therefore got together for a brainstorming session, making full use of the senior IT professional. Together they had come up with a proposal which seemed worthy of closer examination.

The idea was to have a customer information point just inside the door of the supermarket. All regular customers would be given a machine-readable card (like a credit card) or an identification number which they could easily enter into the system when they arrived. On first using the system, customers would enter details of the size of their family, dietary constraints and preferences, and the average weekly food budget to which they would like to work.

On subsequent visits the system would recall this information from memory. The customer would specify how many days' shopping he or she was planning to do on that visit. The system would take account of which days of the week these were (because we like to eat differently at the weekends), and the current stock of items, including those on special offer as a result of bulk-buying from the fresh food market. The system would then produce one or more suggested menus for the coming days, identify the food needed, and provide a map of where these items could be found in the supermarket. This would be helpful to the customer, but would not totally remove the opportunity for impulse buying, which is quite important in this type of retail environment.

The idea sounded interesting but the management team was not confident enough to press ahead as an act of faith. Fortunately, its members got round to reading Chapter 5 of the book just in time. They realized that they shouldn't be taking leaps of faith in this way, but instead should try to sharpen up the business case.

Clearly this was not a *must-do* system; no one required them to make this investment. So the management team had a meeting to discuss the potential benefits in more detail, and began by brainstorming the possible benefits. The resulting list of possible benefits included:

1 Improved company image.
2 Increased customer base.
3 Better knowledge about customers.
4 Increased sales.
5 Increased profit margin.

One senior and enthusiastic manager considered this to be an adequate basis for an *Act of faith* investment. Fortunately he did not have authority to proceed on his own, and his colleagues persuaded him they should try to sharpen up the business case.

First they looked for the *Causal logic* which would explain how these benefits would arise from the introduction of the system. They came up with these main reasons:

(a) *Improved company image.* Most customers are housewives, who meet each other and chat quite regularly. The word would therefore get around that our store was really hi-tech and different; it tried to make things easier for the busy and harassed housewife, instead of just taking her money at the end of the check-out queue. This must surely be a caring company.

(b) *Increased customer base.* The free publicity among customers and their friends would attract more people. The system would also of course be given a big dose of publicity on launch and kept in the public eye. People would be attracted by curiosity, as well as recommendations of existing customers. Once they had tried the system, there would be a good chance that they would find the system useful and they would become longer-term customers.

(c) *Better knowledge about customers.* Gradually the system would build up a useful database about the customers, both individually and collectively. We would know more about the local dietary preferences and shopping habits, enabling us to plan the buying, and the staffing of the shop, more efficiently.

(d) *Increased sales.* There would be a high probability that customers would act upon the tailored advice they were given, and thus sales would increase.

(e) *Increased profit margin.* Because the system would take account of bulk-purchase prices, it could recommend menus with ingredients on which the store would make a greater margin. This would increase average profit levels. Moreover the greater throughput of customers would mean that overheads, as a proportion of sales, would be lower and thus the profit margin higher.

This was beginning to make more business sense. So the management team went on to define how it would be able to *Monitor the direction of change*. This was a matter of identifying business-related quantities which could be measured before and after introduction of the system. The team came up with the following:

1   *Improved company image.* We could conduct random market surveys, to measure public awareness of the system and use of our store. We could count the number of mentions in the local press (apart from our own advertisements of course) to see what interest the system had generated.

2 *Increased customer base.* The system itself would provide, perhaps for the first time, the identity and numbers of existing customers and the way the customer base built up. We can also count people coming through the door, and monitor the number in the store at any one time. This tells us how long people are staying.
3 *Better knowledge about customers.* Again this would come directly from the system, and would probably replace much less reliable survey data.
4 *Increased sales.* Extra sales can be measured direct from the existing POS system, to give a detailed profile through each day of the week.
5 *Increased profit-margin.* This also will come from existing accounting systems for the store.

To *Monitor the size of change* the management team needed to attach numbers to each of these observable, objective quantities. Now it was beginning to get difficult! However, two of the estimates that it came up with after much debate were:

- The throughput of customers in the store (people per day) would increase by 10 per cent.
- Each customer would, on average, spend 10 per cent more. However, there would be a significant number of people who came just to see the system, and then bought nothing.

The team next tried to *Assess the value of change.* Was it better to have more customers coming into the store, or to have each customer buy more? This provoked a long, and at times fairly heated, debate. There was a marketing view that getting people through the door had to be the top priority. Once they had come through the door, the brilliant loss-leader, display, and impulse-buying tactics would simply ensure that the store would do better. However, there was a contrary view that our store shouldn't be full of people who were merely there from idle curiosity, that this did nothing to enhance our reputation, and we did not want to displease our established customers with crowded conditions, queues to use the system, and the ambience of an open-air market. Eventually a consensus was reached: we wanted to keep the average spend up, and not be so concerned about the total numbers coming through the door.

The management team then commissioned more detailed studies to *Assess the financial impact of change.* This showed that in fact the increase in numbers of people in the store had a more direct impact on profit than trying to persuade the same number of people to buy more. Once the figures had been argued through, they swayed the argument back again: we should go for volume. The marketing experts immediately pointed to their superior insight at an earlier stage of the debate. Others bit their tongues and accepted the message from the figures.

This example shows how considerable perseverance and an open mind are needed to sharpen up the business case. Only some of the benefits could, in the end, be translated into hard financial terms. Others could be tested objectively, but it was too tenuous to translate the change into an immediate financial benefit. At the end of the day the management team felt it had a much clearer view of the benefits from the proposed system, and had made the more rational business decision.

Example: marketing system

In the above example it was relatively easy to identify the measures which were to serve as indicators of improved business performance, and then to observe them to see whether the introduction of the information system did indeed have a beneficial effect. It is not always this easy. Sometimes the indicators are subject to variations over which you have little or no control. In that case you are never sure whether an improvement is because of (or in spite of) the introduction of the system. In addition, if the indicators get worse, then you still don't know whether this is in spite of (or even because of) the introduction of the system. This is a serious problem for management, so let's look more closely at it by way of a second example.

This time our company manufactures flavoured yogurts and cold drinks based on dairy products. We produce value-added products based on a commodity (milk). There are several types of retail outlet for our products: national chains of supermarkets (like the previous example), small local chains of supermarkets, and local independent shops. The margins are low (just a few per cent), because the national supermarket chains have used their overwhelming purchasing power to drive down prices at the national level. Moreover the taste for our products varies, and demand depends significantly on the weather.

The board wants to make the most of a rather difficult market. It has conceived the idea of building up a marketing database on a minicomputer to give it an edge over the competition. Instead of just having weekly or monthly totals of sales for each type of outlet, the computer will be able to hold the detailed daily figures for several years past. It will then be possible to perform statistical analysis on this data, and to summarize it in almost any conceivable way. This sounds like a great marketing opportunity, but how are we going to justify the quite substantial investment necessary?

An *Act of faith* would leave it at that level of detail, simply believing that the investment 'has to be right for the company'. Few managers now would be so naive. To get some *Causal logic* we must identify *how* the business will benefit. The board identified these two possibilities:

1   Check in detail what the product line profitability (PLP) is for each product

and each type of outlet. We can then concentrate on the more profitable business activities, and thus increase profit.

2   Correlate the sales data with historical data about the weather in each part of the country. When we know the statistical relationship (if any), then we can use weather forecast as an aid to forecasting market demand. We can then optimize the production of perishable commodities with a strict sell-by or use-by date.

Now both of these benefits are uncertain until we have the system in operation and can determine the facts with confidence. Even then we shall not know how much the business will benefit from our creative use of the data. This is a not uncommon situation: a considerable investment is needed just to know in detail what is going on in the business now. Only then will we have the opportunity to understand what is happening and decide how we might improve things.

In this case the board asked for some very tentative estimates, by the relevant product managers, to get a feel for whether the system was worthwhile. It could then decide whether to press ahead with a full system, try to carry out a pilot system, or forget the whole idea. In our case the board decided on a pilot system. It would be PC-based, and would occupy about three people for 3 months. The board viewed this as a fairly high-risk exploratory investment, and let it be known that this was their view.

Because the system was market-oriented, it would *Monitor the direction of change* by observing sales. However, because of the narrow margins and the fluctuating nature of the business, it would be difficult to know whether changes were caused by the introduction of the system, or were the result of other variables. Basically there are just three approaches to gaining confidence about cause and effect:

(a) To observe the effect over a long period of time, so that the effect of other variables is smoothed out. Thus if market-share fluctuates from month to month, but over the course of a year rises by 20 per cent, then we can be fairly confident we are doing things right. Using a quantity such as market share, rather than an absolute figure such as sales, means that you are observing yourself against the industry norm. You are in fact smoothing out the effects of moves made elsewhere in the industry.

(b) To do a statistical test, by using and then withdrawing the system in a set pattern over the course of a year. Statistical analysis could then be used to sort out whether there is a cause–effect relation between use of the system and the observed business changes. There are well-established techniques for this.

(c) To do a comparative trial, to try to eliminate the effect of the external variables. For example, one product line would use the system to support its marketing, and a similar product line in the same market would not be given use of the system. Any difference in the performance of the two product lines would then be assumed to be due to the effect of the system itself.

These methods are all used in science and engineering, to sort out cause and effect when the 'effect' is masked by extraneous factors. For example, in radar systems the problem is to sort out the target's radio echo from all the radio noise coming from other sources.

In the business context there are other, practical constraints. Method (a) often takes too long; in the course of a year too much may have changed in the business environment for the results to be of much use to influence future planning. Method (b), although it can shorten timescales, would be a nightmare for managers. They would be constantly changing business procedures, as they introduced and withdrew the system. Method (c), though, can be practical in many situations.

Our board opted for the pilot trial, comparing the performance of two similar product lines in one region of the country (to make the comparison as valid as possible). The project had to be handled sensitively, so that those with the system saw it as an opportunity and a challenge, and those without the system did not feel deprived or neglected. In fact their contribution to the success of the trial would be as important as that of their colleagues trying the new system.

Assuming the trial was successful, the board would have greater confidence to introduce the system more widely. Experience from the trial would enable it to sharpen up the business case, to estimate the *size, value,* and *financial impact* of the changes brought by the system.

This example shows how a comparative trial or pilot can be used to get over one of the barriers in sharpening up the business case: sorting out the benefits in the face of extraneous variables. Incidentally, the two benefits which the board was seeking are quite realistic. Using detailed POS and market data has enabled many companies to determine product line profitability for the first time. The retailer Boots did this with its POS system, and as a result was quickly able to decide to drop certain lines, e.g. pet-food, from its shops. The second benefit was to use weather data to forecast demand for perishable goods and thus avoid over- or under-production for the market. Ice cream, beer and soft drinks are examples of other products where this can be done.

The investment culture

So far in this chapter we have concentrated on sharpening up the business case for information systems. The purpose behind this has been to test out the logic which supports the investment decision, identify (and if possible quantify) the benefits in a way which can be observed objectively, and attribute some financial or other value to those benefits. This all makes good sense, but there is another factor to consider – the investment culture of the organization. The business case has to be assembled and presented in a way which matches the procedures for making investment decisions.

The first question to ask is whether IT/IS is a special case. In the past, organizations have often dealt with it as a special case, for a number of reasons:

(a) The subject of IT/IS is highly technical, with a jargon that is impenetrable to the majority of managers. There is therefore a tendency to rely on the recommendations of the specialists, and fail to bring critical management judgement to bear.

(b) The technology is moving fast, and cumbrous decision procedures must not be seen to be holding up investment decisions which might be vital to the future of the company.

(c) We rely on vendors or consultants, and are in a weak position to appraise their recommendations.

As the technology and our management thinking about it mature, there is less of an argument for singling out IT/IS as a special case. An investment in IT should be assessed in the same way, and with the same rigour, as an investment in any other management and business resource. Many managers will nod assent to that statement, but the practice in their organizations may not bear them out. Indeed it is now claimed that sometimes IT/IS is given harsher treatment than other investment decisions, simply because so much management attention has recently become focused upon it.

Thus investment culture for IT/IS should ideally be the same as for other resource areas – neither more nor less demanding. Top management must be able to take a balanced view of all investments, neither neglecting nor giving undue prominence to any one area. Is this so in your organization?

Having identified the investment culture, the sponsor of an IS project may find it necessary to 'package' the proposals so that they will be acceptable to that culture, and stand a fair chance of approval. The commonest example of this is the cost-focused investment culture. Here, it is unlikely that a project will be approved unless it can demonstrate savings. This culture, as we have seen, is not appropriate to many new applications of IT/IS, but nevertheless it persists quite widely. It is especially prevalent in the public sector, where strict cash limits may be in operation and there is little or no scope for entrepreneurial investment.

In such an investment culture it may be necessary to reduce the 'effectiveness' or 'strategic' goals of the system, so that the 'efficiency' benefits alone will make a compelling business case. The effectiveness and strategic benefits will be graciously noted in passing, but will not significantly add to the weight of the business case.

Such packaging of proposals is really a matter of organizational tactics. It should be done only if it is not possible to shift the investment culture to a more enlightened or liberal one that recognizes all three generic benefits of IT/IS.

Thus our recommended approach to the business case for IT/IS investment can be summarized as follows:

1   Recognize the 'must-do' category, and deal with it promptly without wasting effort.
2   Use the six milestones to sharpen up the business case.
3   Identify, and if possible liberalize, the investment culture. Make sure that IT/IS is handled in a similar way to other investments.
4   If necessary, package proposals so that they match the investment culture, even if this means reducing the more strategic or softer benefits.

How does this approach relate to other current management thinking? The work on information economics by Parker and Benson (1988) implicitly uses stages of sharpening up the case. It identifies which benefits can be quantified accurately enough to be aggregated before being put into conventional methods of assessing investment, such as net present value (NPV), payback period, or internal rate of return (IRR). It assesses separately, and places a value judgement upon, the softer benefits. These are added to the equation last. Thus eventually a single figure of merit is reached. That process, although attractive in principle, has the danger of leading people to push the figures too far. Many managers believe that the full range of benefits of IT/IS simply cannot be handled in a mechanistic way leading to a single figure of merit, whether financial or otherwise.

Reimann (1990) has developed the topical concept of value management. A central idea of this is that the external world (particularly the stock market) values a company by its future cash dividends or cash-flow return on investment (CFROI). The company as a whole, or any major business activity within it, must offer a CFROI above the cost of capital, otherwise investment cannot be justified. This approach has implications for corporate investment culture; it requires managers to think in the way that potential investors will think, rather than in strictly internal management terms. It is the marketing principle applied to the equity stakeholder as customer.

The investment culture can therefore be highly oriented towards savings (the oldest, easiest, and most risk-averse approach), or it may be oriented to growth and performance. If the latter, then there will need to be a way of balancing risk and return (as with other portfolios). A simple way to do this is to reserve:

(a) 90 per cent of the available investment budget for cases where simple financial criteria like IRR can be met.
(b) The remaining 10 per cent for approval by top management for higher-risk, less quantified investment based on its judgement.

Enterprises need to recognize these two classes of investment, and that they apply to IT/IS as well as to other resource areas. It is only then that the idea of a portfolio of IT/IS investments, covering all the generic benefits, can be applied sensibly. Otherwise sponsors of projects may find themselves compelled to make weak financial cases, or to package proposals to fit the culture. Either way it can lead to lost opportunity.

A more detailed approach to the problem of portfolio investment is offered by the OTR consulting group and has been reported by Cane (1990). It is called the IT investment grid. On one axis the size of the investment is assessed as low or high; on the other axis the risk of the investment is assessed as low or high. The high/high category is called 'turnaround' and would be approved only if it were vital to the future of the company or business activity. It is suggested that an entrepreneurial company might have 20 per cent of its investment in this category, and 25 per cent in the low/low category. A grid of this kind therefore enables you to consider the IT/IS investment portfolio, and make sure it is balanced in the light of business circumstances.

Whatever your investment culture, it needs to:

• Be consistent for different types of investment, including IT/IS.
• Recognize both hard and soft benefits.
• Balance risk and return.

Taking stock

It is now time for you to take stock of what we have covered in this chapter, by doing Part 4 of the information audit on you and your organization. The questions are shown in Figure 5.3.

Be honest, and if you need to check the thinking behind any of the questions, look back over the relevant part of this chapter.

References

Cane, A. (1990), 'Technique designed to justify IT investment', *Financial Times*, 12 March, p. 32.
Parker, M. and Benson, R. (1988), *Information Economics*, Prentice-Hall, Englewood Cliffs, New Jersey.

Guideline: Identify the benefits, and their value			
Ser.	**Question**	**Score**	**Action**
1	Is the information strategy a peg in the ground for IS planning?		
2	Does senior management oversee the convergence process of planning?		
3	Do you justify various types of IS according to a consistent set of rules?		
4	Do you recognize, and deal with, the 'must-do' category of IS?		
5	Do you recognize a range of types of business case for IS?		
6	Are numbers used unrealistically, in trying to quantify benefits?		
7	Could you sharpen up the way you make the business case?		
8	Is your investment culture the same for IS as for other resources?		
9	Do you package proposals, in order to match the investment culture?		
10	Do you consciously balance risk and return, for IS investment?		
	TOTALS		

Figure 5.3   *IM audit – Part 4*

Reimann, B.C. (1990), *Managing for Value: A Guide to Value-Based Strategic Management*, The Planning Forum/Basil Blackwell, Oxford.

Weill, P. and Olson, M.H. (1989), 'Managing Investment in Information Technology: Mini Case Examples and Implications', *MIS Quarterly*, Vol. 13, No. 1, pp. 2–17 (March).

6 Managing the achievement of the benefits

Introduction

Chapter 5 was mainly about sharpening up the business case, to justify investment in particular IT/IS projects. For some senior managers in some organizations, this might be the end of the story until they heard that the system they had approved had come into operation. Or it might be that the next they hear is that the project is delayed and over budget. Remember the dreadful warning of the IT/IS formula (Figure 2.3). There has to be a better way to do things, to make sure that the benefits identified in the business case are actually achieved in practice. That is what this chapter is about.

The foundation for managing the achievement of the benefits is the IM partnership. If the principles discussed in Chapter 2 have been followed, then the right framework should exist. Top managers, middle managers/users and IT professionals will all have played their part in the planning and approval stage. Now, during implementation, they all have a role as well. You, as the senior manager, need to oversee the total process, as well as make your own particular contribution.

What is an information system?

This is not a formal academic textbook, so I have avoided pedantic definitions. However, the very term 'information system' is open to different interpretations, and we need to be clear what we mean by it. Figure 6.1 offers a definition.

The definition is rather long and boring. It relates to what should properly be called a 'business information system' rather than just an 'information system'. The key functions of the business information system are to collect, store, process and communicate information for the benefit of those people who need to take decisions and initiate action. The key distillation of the

INFORMATION SYSTEM	A collection of procedures, activities, people, and technology set up for the COLLECTION of relevant data, its STORAGE until it is required, its PROCESSING to help provide answers to a specific set of questions, and the COMMUNICATION of the resulting information to the people who need to act upon it.

PEOPLE * PROCEDURES * TECHNOLOGY

Figure 6.1 *Definition of information system*

definition is at the bottom of Figure 6.1: a business information system comprises *people, procedures* and *technology*.

When you use the term information system, this is what you, as a senior general manager, should have in mind. You should always see it in the context of the business and the people who make the business work. That system needs to be designed and managed as a whole.

Unfortunately many of your colleagues will have a narrower perspective of the term information system. For them the term will mean computers, communication systems, software and all the other impedimenta of the technology. Many IT professionals have that narrower view, and you must discourage it. Consider two examples:

- A simple one first. The IS department provides a personal computer and spreadsheet software to a marketing executive, so that he can keep records of sales and a database of his clients. For the IS department the information system may be no more than the PC, the package, and the documentation. The department will expect to give some training and support to the user so that he or she can get used to working the machine and using the package. For the user the information system is about his work – the clients, the sales, the targets, the performance measures against which he will be judged as a marketing executive. The PC and spreadsheet are just tools to help him handle the information better. He doesn't just want advice about the mechanics of the PC; he wants advice from someone who understands (or who is prepared to learn) about the business problems he faces, and what he is trying to achieve.

- An electronic office system is installed and operated by the IS department. It comprises a local area network (LAN), terminals at most desks, interface with external communication systems, and host computers which provide network services to users. This is a highly complex assembly, which is a technical challenge to the IT professionals to install, commission and operate. For the users, though, the system is rather different. It is a new-fangled piece of technology which they may see as threatening or they may welcome for the new opportunites it is said to open up. In either case confidence can be undermined if the system does not come smoothly into operation, is unreliable, or is incomprehensible. And anyway, people say, how will it change our methods of working, now that everyone can send anything to anybody else? Perhaps it would be best to stick to the familiar paper-based system?

In these two examples both viewpoints are valid up to a point. But as a senior manager you must try to embrace both.

Many surveys have shown that there is little correlation between the level of investment which an enterprise makes in IT/IS and its business success, largely because many businesses have taken too narrow a view of the role of IT/IS, and used it simply to automate and speed up the existing business procedures. Automating a bad business process will only make things worse. Automating a good business process will make things better. Using IT/IS as an enabler of new and better business processes is the really smart trick.

The phrase 'people, procedures and technology' echoes the three-stage justification of the information strategy and the three-level specification which it contains (see page 65 and Figure 4.15). Let's now carry that broader view through to the implementation of individual IT/IS projects.

Managing the project

There is a large amount of literature about implementing information systems in the narrow sense. There has been less said about implementing information systems in the wider sense we have just defined. As a starting point, though, we can consider the narrower definition: how to implement an IT/IS project, comprising computer hardware, telecommunication systems, software and other arcane matters which the IT professionals understand and we don't.

Figure 6.2 shows a simple approach to the implementation of an IT/IS project.

There are plenty of academic and proprietary methodologies for implementing projects. See, for example, Davis and Olson (1985), Burch and Grudnitski (1986) and Daniels and Yeates (1988). The essential steps of most approaches are reflected in the six-phase approach of Figure 6.2. There are three phases

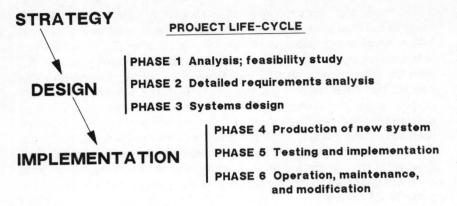

STRATEGY

DESIGN

IMPLEMENTATION

PROJECT LIFE-CYCLE

PHASE 1 Analysis; feasibility study

PHASE 2 Detailed requirements analysis

PHASE 3 Systems design

PHASE 4 Production of new system

PHASE 5 Testing and implementation

PHASE 6 Operation, maintenance, and modification

Figure 6.2   *Project implementation*

associated with project design, and three associated with project implementation. Together they make up the project life-cycle. Let's look briefly at the six phases:

Phase 1 is an analysis of the business situation which the IT/IS project is intended to support. It will include consultation with the management responsible for that business function, and with the people who would be the users of the system if and when it is implemented. It will identify the type of functionality which they will require from the system to support their work to best effect. When this is clear to the analysts, they can see whether the project is feasible, and, if so, prepare an outline specification with approximate costs. This phase is often called the *feasibility study*. It leads to a submission to the steering committee or other body responsible for authorizing the project to proceed. The structure of that submission could well follow the structure of an information strategy (Figure 4.15), but is at a more specific level of detail, concerned with a particular project supporting a particular business function or area.

Phase 2 is the *detailed requirements analysis*. Here the business situation and the functionality required by the users are defined in closer detail. This analysis provides the specification, or user requirement, for the system. It is a very important document. The users (collectively and individually) and the IT professionals must sign it off as the agreed statement of the requirement. Reaching such formal agreement is often a prolonged process; it will require several iterations, as users moderate demands or consider new options and the IT professionals get to understand better the nature of the business problem their system has to support.

Phase 3 is concerned with *systems design*, which is mainly the responsibility of the IT professionals. It translates the functionality specified in the user requirement into the detailed hardware, software and other technology which should provide that functionality. The design will take account of existing systems, and policies defined in the company's information strategy, concerned for example with IT infrastructure, adoption of standards, and compatibility with existing systems. When the design work is complete, the project can go to production. Competitive tendering by a number of possible suppliers may then be asked for.

Phase 4 starts the process of implementation. It is concerned with *production of the new system*, to the specification formalized in Phase 3. Production will usually comprise procurement or manufacture of hardware, procurement or development of software, and the systems integration which makes sure that the various elements work together effectively. This work is usually done in the factory, or at least away from the users' locations.

Phase 5 comprises *testing and implementation*: installation at the users' locations, installing supporting equipment, connecting them to each other and to existing systems, and testing the system out against the user requirement. The users are again consulted, to see that the correct interpretation of the user requirement is given, and that they are happy to accept the system formally.

Phase 6 happens after such formal acceptance of the system by the users. It is concerned with the *operation, maintenance, and modification* of the system to ensure its successful operation and evolution to meet changing user needs. It is a technical support role, usually carried out by the information systems department.

This project life-cycle, comprising six sequential stages, is a methodical approach which incorporates most of the essential aspects of design and implementation of IT/IS projects. Life is rarely that tidy or simple, however! For example, the project life-cycle can be changed in the following ways:

(a) The urgency of the situation may require the phases to overlap, rather than to be strictly sequential. This is analogous to the shortened development and time-to-market pressures of manufacturing industry. There the 'development' and 'production' phases have to overlap if new products are to reach the market in time to compete effectively; the total time has been reduced from 3 years to 9 months in some parts of the fast-moving consumer goods (FMCG) market. Similarly, IT/IS systems have to be developed much more quickly if they are to keep pace with the evolving business situation and the consequent change in user requirements.

(b) Related to this, technical developments with fourth generation languages (4GLs) and integrated product support environments (IPSEs) enable Phases 2 and 3 to be much more interactive. The users and the IT professionals work together, often in front of a VDU screen, to develop the tailored applications which the users are going to find most appropriate to their needs. It is important, though, that this iterative activity still concludes with a formal statement of user requirement, signed off by both parties.

(c) With large projects, or those with complex requirements, it may be too risky to approve implementation without seeing a 'pilot' working version of the system. Pilot projects can be used as another vehicle for iteration between the users and the IT professionals, to make sure the system is as effective as it may be. Sometimes the conventional approach is called the 'V-diagram': it descends from the user requirement, down into the technical detail of design and production, and back up to a working system delivered to the user. The use of a pilot system results in a 'W-diagram': the pilot system comes up part way through the process, for the user to try out to gain confidence about the requirement and the way the IT professionals propose to meet that requirement.

The project life-cycle has to be managed, like any other practical piece of design development and implementation. A 'project' is something unique; it is different from 'production', which is usually repetitive. Projects usually have specific time and budget constraints, defined when they are formally approved. Project teams are often assembled to manage and support them, or they may be formed by temporary responsibilities allocated within a matrix-management system. Either way, tools like the Gantt chart (for time-event planning) and critical path analysis (CPA) will be used to manage the project to successful completion. More details of these management techniques and the six-phase project life-cycle are given in Knight and Silk (1990).

Managing the people

A 'project' approach is essential for the successful design and implementation of an IT/IS system. We have already identified those phases in which the users of the system need to be consulted. In the six-phase approach suggested, this is mainly in Phases 1–2 and 5–6. However, most organizations now recognize that there are wider 'people' aspects associated with IT/IS projects. Taking the broader definition of an information system (to include people, procedures and technology), this is very obvious. It is also very important.

Some of the related issues are listed in the top part of Figure 6.3.

The threats make a daunting list, but remember that they are 'perceived threats', not necessarily real threats. However, the people concerned may perceive them as very real indeed. You, as a manager, must therefore take those perceived threats seriously, and respond sympathetically.

PERCEIVED THREATS

To jobs, status, confidence, the organization, competence, health

MANAGEMENT ACTIONS

Consult, negotiate, familiarize, train, support

Figure 6.3   *People issues*

Most fears are fears of the unknown. People may consider IT/IS to be threatening because they do not understand it, and do not know how it will affect their jobs and lives. Let's look at the kind of fears people have.

Perhaps the biggest fear is the possible loss of a *job*:

> Perhaps the new technology will be able to do my job better than I can. If so, you can bet the management will do away with me just as soon as they can, and then I shall be in a right mess. So I'd better resist the introduction of this new system, or at least not go out of my way to co-operate about it. I dread it when all these clever-dick IT-types come around asking me about how I do my job and how their computers could do things better.

There are fears for *status*:

> The system is going to do all that planning which I've been doing for years. There won't be much left for me to do except put the data in, and take the results out. What are my colleagues going to think? It's a real come-down after all these years when I have been the hub of our production planning department. I suppose they'll re-grade me as a data-entry clerk or something.

Or lack of *confidence*:

> I don't know if I shall be able to cope with this new system they're bringing in. It's all right for the younger people – they got used to keyboards at school and with their computer games at home. You can't teach an old dog new tricks, so I shall just have to try to avoid getting involved with this new system. If they impose it on me, I suppose I'll just make a fool of myself trying to use it. Do you think it could blow up, if I press the wrong keys?

People also realize that new systems, especially networks and office auto-mation systems, will affect not only individual jobs but the way the *organization* as a whole operates:

> With the paper-based system we all knew where we stood. There were well-defined procedures, and it all worked like clockwork. Now, with this electronic system, anyone can send anything to anyone else. We get so much electronic junk mail, and people print out nearly all of it and put it in their filing cabinets. We seem to have more paper than ever before, and I thought these systems were supposed to help us save forests and be more efficient. People seem to bypass the proper channels now, forming little groupings over the network which have nothing to do with the way we're supposed to be organized. It's not like working in a human organization any more – just hour after hour staring at that screen. And that thing that blinks all the time waiting for you to do something – it's taunting you all the time. It makes me guilty just to look at it.

Even if they are not afraid of the technology, they may wonder whether they will be able to acquire the skills and *competence* which the new systems will require:

> It worries me to think what I have got to learn, with this new system. It took me years to get used to the electronic typewriter. That was bad enough, but this new word-processor has so many extra keys and the manual is 3 inches thick. How am I going to learn all that, when the boss is breathing down my neck wanting his dictation printed out to catch the next post? These computer people just assume you can pick it up as you go along, or that you will take those manuals home to study all night. They seem to love their machines, so I expect they take the manuals home and learn them off by heart. I've got other things to do at home.

And there are very real concerns about *health*:

> I've read somewhere that it's just not healthy working all the time with these VDU things. It's all right for the bosses – they just fiddle about with the computer for a few minutes and then rush off to a meeting, or lunch. But we have to sit in front of it all day. I've never had so much backache and eyestrain as since we got the new system. And of course nobody bothered about changing the lighting or making sure we had good office chairs and a suitable desk layout. They just came in and plonked the VDU on top of my desk, just where I used to have the photo of my husband and children. It's a good job we're not planning any more children – these VDU things give off all sorts of rays which aren't good for you if you're pregnant.

Some of these perceived threats are real. The health one is serious: posture, lighting, ergonomics and hazards to pregnant women must all be handled carefully. If you really are putting in a cost-cutting system, seeking savings which threaten people's jobs, there will be little point in pretending otherwise, to yourself or to them. You will need to address the issues of training, new jobs, or possible redundancy early on.

But many of the perceived threats will be unfounded. These you can deal with if you recognize that they exist, and take management action before they become inflated to serious proportions.

How? For any major system, or one which will affect the workstyle of many people, the first step is to make sure that there is a 'product champion' at the top level of the organization. The champion has to be seen as the leader; he or she must exude confidence and enthusiasm about the project, be persuasive, and be influential in the organization. Surveys show that the product champion is the common factor in most successful projects. The principle is the same for any aspect of corporate change, but in this case you need to think carefully who the right champion would be. It will not necessarily be a senior IT professional; indeed surveys have shown that more often than not the most effective champion is a senior business manager who has a clear perspective of the strategic importance of IT/IS.

The bottom part of Figure 6.3 lists the detailed measures you should consider. They sound fairly obvious, like motherhood statements. But it is important that they do happen, and that they happen at the right time in the project life-cycle.

You need to *consult* the people who will be affected by the system, whether they will be direct users of it or not. Initially this will mean a process of *education* – explaining why the system is needed to support the business, to show that other alternatives have been considered (including doing nothing), and to let people involved know that they will be consulted about the details before major decisions are made. You may need to use several means of communication at this stage: team briefings, background articles in the house magazine, open days in the IS department, videos about what the general practice in your industry has become. It is all about reassuring people, to allay their worst fears and to encourage them to participate in the development of a system which will be better for them and better for the business. In essence, it is extending the IM partnership to include *all* the people who will be affected by the system; it is the first step in a culture change in attitude towards the new system which you have in mind.

During Phases 1 and 2, when users are consulted about their business processes and the functionality they need from the system, there will be much more listening to be done. The people conducting these discussions may be insiders (from the IS department) or outsiders (consultants or vendors). In either case they need to be sensitive not only to the formal agenda (defining user requirements) but also the hidden agenda (obliquely implying support, fear or resistance to the project). There may be individuals who need particular care and attention to establish and maintain the right climate. There may be organized groups, such as trade unions, with whom you will need to *negotiate* about the introduction of the system, the training needed, and any changes to pay scales resulting from the new way of working. All this needs to be done at this early stage of the project; delay engenders suspicion and gives objectors a powerful weapon – to defer the use of a system already committed to production.

The middle phases of a lengthy project have particular dangers. People have forgotten the initial publicity and high profile of the project, they have done the sometimes boring task of defining and agreeing requirements, they have been promised jam tomorrow, and now there is nothing to see. The process of education needs to continue: to keep people advised on the progress of the system, to keep it in their minds, and to give them an authoritative view on when they will see it in operation. It is easy for top management and IT professionals, who will be monitoring the progress of the project, to forget that there are many others who can now lose all sight of what is happening.

The final phases (commissioning and operation) need to be planned carefully. You need to *familiarize* people with the equipment and facilities which they will be getting. If you are using a pilot project, then this can act as a mid-project booster. This is the advantage of the W-diagram over the V-diagram for system development discussed on page 88. Familiarization leads naturally into *training*, so that users can be effective when the system comes into operation. Often special provision is made with contractors (or the internal team from the IS department) to have training sessions linked in with the formal commissioning tests of the system. Finally, users will need *support* when the system has come into operation. They will need ongoing training and advice. A 'help' facility (both on-screen and human) is essential. At this stage the experts who have designed and implemented the system know more about it than anyone else; it is important that they don't disappear from the users' view as soon as they hand the system over. This can be a problem when a project team was formed and is now disbanding, or contractors are now leaving site. You need to make provision for continuing support as part of the scope of the formal project.

New systems mean new ways of doing things, and this implies change. As a manager you are used to the problems of handling change, so do not forget the principles in this context. With new information systems you can expect to see the usual four stages in the change process:

(a) *Denying the need for change.* 'It won't really affect me. I shall just quietly get on with things the way I always have. This new system will just be a flash in the pan; it'll never work properly. Why do they always want to change things?'

(b) *Accepting the need for change.* 'Perhaps this system really could help us do things better, and after all if the firm doesn't get more efficient, it will be my job that's on the line. All my friends seem to have accepted that we need to give it a go, so perhaps I'd better get more involved too. If I don't, I might be left behind.'

(c) *Participating in the change.* 'Well, we're in it up to our ears now. There's a lot to learn with the new system, and it's almost impossible to keep the business going at the same time as we make the change. But we can see that it'll probably be worth it in the long run: it should be easier without all those slips of paper we keep losing.'

(d) *Benefiting from the change.* 'I've really got the hang of it now, and things are beginning to settle down a bit. There's no doubt we're quicker and more efficient than we were, and this benefits us and the customers. Why didn't we make this change years ago?'

These are the stages you can expect, even if you have followed all the other good management principles to the full. There will be a drop in morale, and in operating effectiveness, during the second and third of these four stages. This dip is characteristic of any process of change, and you need to be sensitive to it. During the dip try to give extra support and encouragement; try to avoid demoralizing failures of the system or of the support you are giving the users.

All these people aspects of implementing IS projects are vitally important to success. It is easy to overlook or neglect them when there are often more pressing problems relating to the project itself. However, as a senior manager, you need to keep both aspects in view – defining not only the 'project milestones' of implementation but also 'people milestones' to ensure that users are prepared, motivated and equipped to use the system in the way intended, and are supported during the subsequent process of change.

Managing the benefits

The project milestones and people milestones are shown in the first two columns of Figure 6.4. Most modern organizations recognize these two types of milestone, even if they are not wholly effective in achieving them. What is less common, but increasingly necessary, is to integrate the management of the benefits from the IT/IS project into the same development life-cycle. Thus we have a third theme to the management of IS, with benefit milestones alongside the other two. Just as the people milestones ensure that the users are prepared for the system, so benefit milestones ensure that the business benefit will flow from the way the people use the system. Let's look briefly at the principles here.

In Chapter 5 we saw how the business case could be sharpened up, to make it as quantified and business-oriented as possible. The proposed method enables you to take a coherent view of both hard (tangible) and soft

MANAGE		
PROJECT	**PEOPLE**	**BENEFITS**
DESIGN 1 Initial analysis 2 User requirement 3 Systems design	Educate Consult/negotiate	Identify Justify
IMPLEMENTATION 4 Production 5 Installation/test	Train	
OPERATION 6 Opn, maint, modifn	Support	Monitor/review

Figure 6.4   *IS management*

(intangible) benefits. That discussion was in the context of assembling the business case for the project as a whole. What we now need to do is adopt the same principles at a more detailed level, relating to how individuals use the system.

During Phases 1 and 2 of the project it must not simply be a matter of asking users what they want from the system. They are not likely to know, or they may ask for something quite unrealistic. I suggest you follow three principles here:

(a) Make sure there is an iterative discussion between the users and those who know the scope and capability of the technology. Make sure the user understands the technical opportunity, and the technician understands the business context, at the level of the individual user.
(b) Get the user to identify the business benefit which he or she will derive from the functionality being asked for in the user requirement. In effect there must be a business case, based on the principles of Chapter 5, for each user (or type of user) of the system.
(c) This business benefit and business case must be agreed and 'owned' by the particular user. This will give commitment to achieving the benefit, and (equally important) mean that the user will be prepared to accept responsibility for ensuring that the benefit is really achieved in practice.

The last point is very important. There must be a commitment, or 'contract', between the individual user and management that the system *will* deliver the benefits. You will need to think how that commitment or contract can best be recorded. It might be enough to rely on a shared understanding at the end of Phases 1 and 2. More likely it won't: people move on, or forget (wilfully or otherwise). It might be better to write the business benefits, and the measures to observe them, into the user requirement document. This might affect the system design, to provide the right management measures relating to business success. Alternatively you might have a separate document for individual users or departments. The important point is to have some agreed contract relating the provision of an information facility or service and the deriving of specific business benefit as a result.

Sometimes this can be given a clear focus by running the IS department as a profit-centre, so that the individual user (or user department) can contract with the IS department for the provision of the new service, at an agreed price. This should result in a service level agreement (SLA) which specifies what is being provided. The need to pay for the SLA out of individual or departmental operational budgets is then an immense incentive for the user to think through the business case for himself!

The contract, in whatever form, then becomes one aspect of an individual's job description. He or she accepts responsibility for making it happen. It can therefore be absorbed into the normal process of individual appraisal and review. In this way it is firmly on the individual user's agenda for action.

This links to the second major principle of what we have called benefit management. There should be a process of monitoring and review after the system comes into operation, to make sure that the 'contracts' are being fulfilled and the business benefits achieved. This process should be seen as a natural part of the management of the total information system (people, procedures and technology). It should not be a separate *ad-hoc* audit. Still less should it be a retrospective witch-hunt when senior management, having forgotten or neglected the project since approving it some time ago, suddenly becomes aware that things are not turning out quite as it had hoped and intended. There may be failure, and there may be good reasons for failure, but you need to be able to review these in a controlled manner by reference to documented intention and commitment.

Monitor and review can then become part of the IM partnership between users and the business, and not come to be perceived as adversarial. Difficulties and failure will not be pleasant, but at least make sure that you are all standing together to face the problems, rather than facing each other in mutual recrimination.

Make sure, then, that you manage project, people, and benefits in parallel. Most organizations manage the first two; many neglect the third, and it can undo much of what might otherwise be achieved.

Finally, let's illustrate these principles of benefit management in the context of the two examples which we looked at in Chapter 5: the customer information point for the retail supermarket and the marketing database for the producer of value-added milk products. You might need to refresh your memory about these two examples, from pages 72–76 and 76–78 respectively.

In the retail supermarket case the management team went through all the steps of sharpening up the business case, and came to the conclusion that the customer information point would give the best benefit by increasing the number of customers rather than by trying to persuade each customer to buy more. There would be several people who would have to take responsibility for achieving the five benefits the team had identified:

1 *Improved company image.* The firm's local PR manager would take responsibility for promoting the new system (other than by direct advertisement), for monitoring the mentions in the press, and for conducting market surveys to determine increased awareness of the firm and this particular feature. These objectives can and should be quantified.
2 *Increased customer base.* The firm's local marketing manager would take responsibility for paid advertisements, monitoring the numbers of people entering the store, and (from the system) their identities. He can then monitor the size of the customer base, in relation to the targets he has accepted.
3 *Better knowledge about customers.* Again, the marketing manager would be responsible for analysing the new data about the customers and their shopping needs, and identifying new opportunities, e.g. lines not yet offered.
4 *Increased sales.* The floor manager might be responsible for maximizing sales, to take advantage of the new style of dealing with customers, and the increased numbers in the shop. He would be responsible for the knowledge base which the computer used to make recommendations in response to dietary requirements, making sure that the store's full product line was promoted to good effect.
5 *Increased profit margin.* The buyer would be responsible for adapting the product range to match the customer profile more closely. He would take advantage of special offers he could get, without necessarily passing on the saving to the customer. If the customer is satisfied, the margin can be higher.

All these individuals will be responsible for achieving their respective business benefits from the new system. They should each be persuaded that they can get the benefit, and then work to achieve it. In addition, there will need to be a management overview as part of the monitoring process. There may sometimes be conflicting requirements to resolve, e.g. regarding throughput of customers and the profit margin.

In the case of the marketing database for dairy products there were two objectives: to identify product line profitabilities (PLPs), and to use statistical analysis to take advantage of weather forecasts. The number of people affected would probably be smaller: the brand manager using the pilot system would undertake to identify the PLPs in greater detail than he does at present. He would use this information to adjust the product range to improve profits over the period of the trial; and he would seek to use the statistical data to match supply and demand more closely, taking account of changes in the weather. His report on the trial of the pilot system would become, in effect, the business case for investment in wider use of the system.

Taking stock

This chapter has continued the process of 'convergence' started in Chapter 5. It has taken the issues to the level of individual users (or sets of users), and of individual IT/IS projects. The principles of the business case, already developed for the information strategy and for the project as a whole, have now been applied at the more detailed level. The result should be that:

- Users have a commitment to the project, and have entered a contract (formal or otherwise) to achieve business results in exchange for the provision of their part of the system.
- Responsibility falls with the user, or group of users, and this can then be managed within the normal framework of responsibility and appraisal.

Guideline: Manage the achievement of the benefits			
Ser.	**Question**	**Score**	**Action**
1	Do you manage information systems as people, procedures and technology?		
2	Do you give the right balance of management attention to these three?		
3	Do you know the project life-cycle, or equivalent, used in your business?		
4	Do you consciously adapt it for urgent or complex cases?		
5	Do you know what threats your people perceive from IT/IS?		
6	Do you take appropriate action, at the right time in the project life-cycle?		
7	Do you consciously practise benefit management for IT/IS?		
8	Are requirements and benefits defined and agreed together, by users?		
9	Is the achievement of the benefits monitored, in subsequent operation?		
10	Does senior management monitor progress, or have witch-hunts afterwards?		
	TOTALS		

Figure 6.5 *IM audit – Part 5*

To achieve this, senior management need to be conscious of the need to manage the project, the people and the benefits in a balanced way. Most organizations now cope with the first two; the successful ones cope with all three.

Inevitably, it is now time for you to take stock of practice in your enterprise in respect of these principles. The ten questions are shown in Figure 6.5, and relate to the various sections of this Chapter. You may need to look back to make sure you understand them correctly.

References

Burch, J. G. and Grudnitski, G. (1986), *Information Systems: Theory and Practice*, 4th Ed, Wiley, New York.

Daniels, A. and Yeates, D. (1988), *Basic Systems Analysis*, 3rd Ed, Pitman, London.

Davis, G. B. and Olson, M. H. (1985), *Management Information Systems: Conceptual Foundations, Structure, and Development*, McGraw-Hill, New York.

Knight, A. V. and Silk, D. J. (1990), *Managing Information*, McGraw-Hill, London.

7 Preparing for the future

Introduction

The six guidelines for information management upon which this book is based are:

1 Establish an information management partnership.
2 Distinguish the potential (generic) benefits of IT/IS.
3 Think strategically about information management.
4 Identify the benefits, and their value.
5 Manage the achievement of the benefits.
6 Prepare for the future.

The first guideline is about establishing the right management framework. The second and third are about broadening the corporate thinking on this subject, so that it becomes closely related to business strategy. This is the 'diverge' part of your collective thinking, and is captured in the information strategy for the organization. The fourth and fifth guidelines 'converge' the discussion, first to the level of the individual IT/IS project and then to the level of the individual user, or group of users. This convergence enables you to define benefits in a business context, allocate responsibility for achieving them, and thus make 'benefit management' part of your normal monitoring and appraisal system. I hope you have found the discussion of Guidelines 1–5 coherent and relevant.

This cannot be a once-and-and-for-all process. The world does not stand still, especially in respect of IT/IS. The purpose of Guideline 6 is to broaden your thinking again, and perhaps start on another diverge–converge sequence which will equip you to take fuller use of the emerging opportunities offered by IT/IS. As a senior manager, you have a special responsibility for monitoring the environment which surrounds your business, including its political, regulatory, competitive, social, technical and many other aspects. You need to spot the opportunities, and then get them tested out by discussion within the organization. In the field of information management and IT/IS things are changing as rapidly as anywhere.

'Prepare for the Future', it says. How can we? Well, in Chapter 4 we've already considered some methods of preparation:

(a) Keep the senior manager's strategic perspective: the 5-year view which 'plans the voyage' for the enterprise as a whole (pages 44–50).
(b) Be aware of the challenge of the business environment, and the particular challenge for information management (pages 50–52).
(c) Take the internal, external, and dynamic views of your enterprise (pages 52–63).
(d) Capture the result of your strategic thinking in an information strategy (pages 63–66).

One management discipline has already been suggested: to review the information strategy every year or so, to check whether the business analysis and logic are still valid. This review is the regular cue to check whether things have changed significantly.

All this is fine, and business-directed. Yet you should also take a broader interest in how IT and its applications are developing, and are likely to further change in the next 10 years or so. This chapter will help you to do that, by taking several different perspectives of the future. It should stimulate your thinking in this area.

A future built on the past

Before taking a look into the future it is always a good idea to look back on the past. So, how long is the history of information technology? The narrow definition of IT is the convergence of computing and telecommunications made possible by modern microelectronics. On that basis it is about 30 years old. In that time it has made remarkable advances both technically and in its impact on business and society. Yet this is scarcely a long enough time to provide a clear historical perspective.

If you take a broader definition of IT, as the use of tools by man to record and communicate information, then it is much older. In fact it is at least 20,000 years old, because that is the age of the remarkable drawings found in the caves of France and Spain, for example. This longer history of IT is shown in Figure 7.1.

The figure shows some of the key events in the 20,000 years since those cave drawings. About 3000 BC formal writing systems were developed, exemplified by the carvings in the Egyptian tombs. These were complex systems of writing, and scarcely practical for everyday use. A more rapid and convenient form of

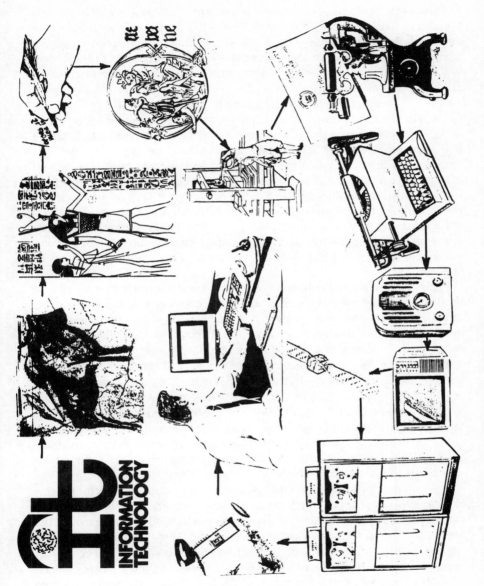

Figure 7.1 *Information technology throughout the ages*

writing was developed, using simpler tools and materials. The hand-written book became the recording medium for much of the world's knowledge, and 'history' in the literal sense was born.

The written book thus became very important as a repository of the human knowledge and culture. Books were decorated artistically, with elaborate illuminations and bindings. The art of the decorated manuscript flourished during the eleventh century, when, in the West, the church was the custodian of the knowledge, and added to the important monopoly of information of the church and its related institutions. The fascinating story of the development of writing has been recounted by, for example, Jackson (1981).

Then in the mid-fifteenth century a major event occurred: the re-invention in the West of the technique of printing from movable type (something which had been practised by the Chinese long before). The impact of this was immense: suddenly the cost, in human effort, of producing a book was reduced from man-years (a human scribe copying a source book) to man-days (for a simple print-shop producing many copies of a book). Moreover the accuracy was greatly increased, and there was total consistency between copies in a given print run. Within about 50 years the new technology became dominant as the mainstay of recording and disseminating information. Moreover it was no longer the monopoly of one institution. This had immense social implications.

Paper-based communication became more important, whether written or printed. Gradually a postal system was developed to deal with this information, and satisfy the increasing demands of trade as physical communications improved. By the nineteenth century the international postal service was established. Paper became the mainstay of business.

Then in the 1830s another technology appeared: Michael Faraday discovered the link between electricity and magnetism, and investigated its practical application. A spectacular series of inventions followed. The electric telegraph was deployed from the 1840s and the telephone from the late 1870s. Meanwhile the typewriter appeared, as an early form of office automation.

In the twentieth century the developments have been even more spectacular. Radio, television and satellites were among major developments in communications. During and after the Second World War the technology of computing developed rapidly. The invention of the integrated circuit (microchip) in 1960 was the beginning of a new era in electronic technology. It vastly increased the speed, reliability and accuracy of electronics, and provided the foundation for modern information technology. This is exemplified by the manager sitting at his desk with access to storage, processing and communication capability which would have been undreamt of a few years earlier.

That is a very abbreviated history of IT/IS, but what are the lessons we note from it? I suggest the following:

- There has been a continuous development in IT/IS, but the last 30 years have provided a notable acceleration in the pace of that development.
- Most progress has been evolutionary, rather than revolutionary. Inventions often occur in several places at about the same time, and it takes some time for their impact to be felt upon the pattern of daily life.
- Among the few technical milestones we can perhaps list:

BC 3000   The invention of writing systems.
AD 1450   Printing from movable type, in the West.
AD 1831   The discovery of electromagnetic induction.
AD 1906   The invention of the thermionic valve.
AD 1948   The invention of the transistor.
AD 1960   The invention of integrated circuits.

Printing has perhaps been the most significant IT development so far, in terms of its widespread impact. In any event, we must be cautious about extravagant claims about the new 'information age' which is said to be about to dawn. It has been a long time a-coming, because the speed of acceptance of new technology is much slower than the speed with which the technical advances are made.

This historical perspective of IT should help you keep a sense of proportion when you listen to the enthusiasts. Equally, you can and should take a historical perspective of the development of IT/IS in your own particular enterprise. You may not be happy with the business procedures used, or the way that IT/IS supports them, but they are the product of your collective wisdom (or lack of it) in the organization. It is worth reflecting on how IT/IS has developed; it may help you diagnose why you are not realizing the full potential of developing technology.

A future built on sand – literally

The future for IT/IS is built upon sand literally, in the sense that sand is the source of two of the major raw materials of modern IT: silicon and glass. Each has already had a strong impact upon IT/IS. Each will continue to make a strong impact, and it is useful for you as a manager to have an overview of the way developments are likely to go.

Silicon technology

First silicon. The development in the complexity of silicon Integrated Circuits is shown in Figure 7.2.

YEAR	COMPONENTS PER CHIP	NAME
1960	10	Small scale integration (SSI)
1965	100	Medium scale integration (MSI)
1970	1,000	Large scale integration (LSI)
1975	10,000	Very large scale integration (VLSI)
1980	100,000	
1985	1,000,000	
1990	10,000,000	Ultra large scale integration (ULSI)

GROWTH: Times ten every 5 years (47% per annum)

Figure 7.2   *VLSI development*

The complexity of microchips has followed an exponential (compound) growth of about 47 per cent per annum for 30 years. Few other technologies can claim such a rapid and sustained development. Very large scale integration (VLSI), with about 10,000 components per chip, has given way to ultra large scale integration (ULSI) with many millions of components per chip. This rate of expansion is not yet approaching the physical limits and can therefore be expected to continue. New techniques etch finer and finer detail on to the surface of the chip, and also use larger areas of silicon, to achieve much more complex chips. Although there are other technologies (such as gallium arsenide) for special high-speed applications, it is generally accepted that silicon will continue to be the mainstay of business computing, and that its remarkable growth will continue for many years yet. An overview of this has been given by Gosling (1988) and Oakley (1990).

What does this more powerful chip technology make possible? It is helpful to look at the aims of the so-called fifth-generation computing system (FGCS) project, which ran from 1981 to 1991 in Japan. Its aims are shown in Figure 7.3.

In 1981 the Japanese stated their research goals for the coming 10-year period in computing. The *hardware* had to develop 100-fold in capacity. This would support new and more complex types of *software*, for example:

(a) Intelligent knowledge-based systems (IKBS) which can capture human 'knowledge' and expertise. The emerging technology of expert systems was an example of this: a few hundred rules expressing knowledge in a particular 'domain' can be formulated by human experts and then stored

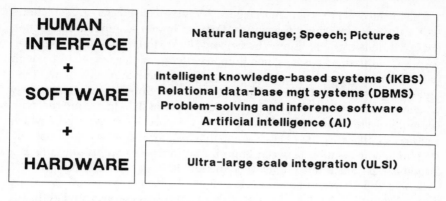

Figure 7.3   *Fifth-generation computing systems (FGCS)*

in a machine. They can then be applied to a variety of particular cases. In some fields the performance of an expert system is better than the performance of individual human experts in the team which formulated the rules for it. More details of expert systems are given in standard texts such as Harmon and King (1985).

(b) More flexible *database* technology, so that data can be retrieved and examined in ways which suit the needs of the user, rather than being constrained by the way in which the data were originally entered. For example, an order-entry system might have data entered by date and part-numbers, but the system might be searched to determine the buying profile and habits of a particular customer over a period of time.

(c) *Software* which solves more realistic types of problems than the step-by-step algorithms of traditional computers (which are very good at logical and mathematical problems, but not so good at 'soft' and fuzzy problems). The software needs to be able to discern and identify relationships in a way similar to that of the human brain. An important aspect of this is in pattern-recognition, which is essential for giving robots the ability to 'see' their environment.

(d) More developed types of software which will not only discern patterns but express the results in the form of rules which are of wider application. This is the inductive method of deriving new knowledge (from the particular to the general) rather than the deductive method (from the general to the particular). Machines which can do this are associated with the term *artificial intelligence* (AI). This is a controversial term, but machine intelligence is perhaps best defined as that behaviour which, in a person, we would call intelligent. In that sense there is no doubt that computers can be intelligent. The philosophical question as to whether machines really 'think' tends to be sterile.

The top level of FGCS shown in Figure 7.3 is the *human interface*, sometimes called the man–machine interface (MMI) or human-computer interaction (HCI). The idea was that human users would like to interact with computers in ways similar to the ways in which humans interact with each other, i.e. with natural language such as English or Japanese (whether spoken or written), and with pictures. It will be a sign of the maturity of computer technology when people don't find that they have to learn special skills just to interact with computer systems and use them effectively. A specific research goal which captured all these aspects of FGCS was a machine for real-time translation of a telephone conversation between English and Japanese. Technically this is a formidable problem, but it illustrates the ambition of the FGCS project.

Besides the 10-year Japanese FGCS effort, there have been corresponding research efforts in the West. In Europe there is the Esprit project, and in the UK the Alvey Programme (1983–8) and its successor, the Joint Framework for Information Technology (JFIT). How far have all these projects succeeded in achieving the FGCS goals?

In terms of hardware (chip) development, they have been wholly successful. The 100-fold increase in 10 years has been achieved. In terms of software development, there have been much more difficult problems – formidable obstacles to achieving FGCS goals. Important advances in man–machine interface have been achieved, however. A simple example is the graphical user interface (GUI) and 'mouse', now widely used with personal computers.

Software, and our understanding of the mechanisms of the human mind, seem to be the bottlenecks at present. One promising line of research is 'neural networks', which are an electronic replication of the kind of interconnected elements of which the human brain is built up. Instead of programming a computer to carry out a series of steps, you 'teach' the computer by exposing it to a range of named stimuli; it can then succeed in recognizing the same, or similar, stimuli in the future. Thus computers can now recognize faces quite reliably in this way. It is unnecessary to understand the detailed mechanisms by which they do it; the machine 'learns' to do something useful, rather than having to be told in detail how to solve a problem. The term sixth-generation computing systems has been coined for neural networks of this kind.

So much for the continuing advances in *silicon* technology, and the new systems which it makes possible. What about the second major product of sand, namely *glass?*

Glass technology

Electrical/electronic technology has been used for handling information since the 1840s. There is no special reason why electrical technology should have a monopoly for this, however. Indeed, in the nineteenth century Babbage was experimenting with his 'analytical engine', which used mechanical technology to perform information processing. Today there is a significant move from electrical to optical technology. The data or pieces of information are still handled as pulses (commonly called 0s and 1s, or 'bits'), but the pulses can be flashes of light rather than surges of electrical current. Optical technology has an immense capacity, and it is important to understand its full potential.

The smallest practical measure of information is the 'byte', which contains eight bits and is used to represent a single alphanumeric character like 'Q' or '3'. To put this into perspective:

1   An A4-page of typescript has about 2,000 bytes, usually called 2 kilobytes (2K).
2   One second's worth of high-quality telephone speech requires 8,000 bytes, or 8K.
3   One second's worth of colour television, if coded efficiently, requires about 1,000,000 bytes, or one megabyte (1M).

These figures illustrate three important points: text, as stored in a word-processor, is a very efficient way of handling information; voice requires much more capacity; and images (particularly moving pictures) require a lot more capacity still. This explains why we still have relatively few picturephones and videoconferencing links in use.

Optical technology, based upon glass, has two well-established areas of application, and one which is likely to take longer to reach practical fruition:

(a) *Optical communication* is done over fibre optic cables (FOCs) made of very thin strands of high-purity glass encased in a protective sheath. The information is sent as pulses of light; at each end there is a conversion to and from the electrical form used by the rest of the communication system. Since the mid-1980s FOC has been the mainstay of fixed terrestrial communication, both on land and increasingly for submarine communication cables. There is now a circle of fibre around the world. The operating speed of these FOC systems is increasing steadily. A fibre can carry about 35,000 voice channels simultaneously; in terms of data this corresponds to the text of the *Bible* in 1/100 sec. or the text of the *Encyclopedia Britannica* in 4 sec. FOC is releasing the radio spectrum for use by satellite and mobile radio systems.

(b) *Optical storage* can be done with the same technology as is used in a domestic compact disc (CD), where the information is written and read by a laser. A standard CD can now hold 600 megabytes (600M) of data, which is as much as the hard-disk capacity of at least twelve modern PCs. To get some perspective of the trends in storage capacity, consider the upper limit of how much data could be stored in the volume represented by a cube with 12in. (30cm) sides

(i) With *paper*, you could get about 2,500 A4 sheets. Text on both sides of every sheet would give about 10 megabytes (10M) of capacity.

(ii) With *photographic*, *integrated-circuit* or *magnetic* storage, you could get about one gigabyte (1G), which is a hundred times as much.

(iii) With digital *optical* storage, you could get about 400 gigabytes (400G). This is equivalent to 4,000 filing cabinets full of paper, 1.6 years of speech, or 4.6 days of non-stop TV. Exhausting indeed!

(c) *Optical processing* is still in the research stage. Potentially it could enable information to be handled entirely optically within a system, instead of it having to be converted to and from an electrical form. The speeds of today's computing systems could be increased 1,000-fold.

The figures are difficult to grasp, but it is clear that IT will continue to show remarkable developments of speed and capacity. Moravec (1988) has examined the development of computing technology since the 1940s and predicts that within 20 years (by 2010) a supercomputer will be available with the capacity of the human brain; and within 40 years (by 2030) this capacity will be available in a device the size and cost (in real terms) of today's personal computer.

The implications of this rapidly expanding technology are immense. What other management resource is expanding in power so rapidly, and at the same time decreasing in cost? It is likely that whatever *can* be done with IT eventually *will* be done with IT. But how quickly? This leads us to our third perspective of the future.

A future built on sand – metaphorically

The big questions are not about IT, but about how we will use it and whether we can cope with it. To get our minds round this, let's take a gradually broadening view of this aspect of the problem, starting with the human brain and working up to the level of human society.

IT and the brain

The human brain contains about 10 billion (10,000,000,000) neurons, each connected to about 10,000 others. This immensely complex configuration can, in principle, store the equivalent of 100,000 gigabytes, much greater than the storage capacity of even the largest of today's supercomputers. It is enough to store continuous moving images for the duration of our entire lifetime. There is evidence that more is stored in our brains than we can consciously recall. What we call 'learning' is perhaps more accurately described as 'establishing a recall facility'. Nevertheless our common experience is that we have to make a conscious effort to commit to long-term memory things which we handle routinely in our short-term memory. An example is how we remember a telephone number. We may look it up in the directory or in our notebook and remember it for the few seconds which it takes us to dial the number. But if we need to redial we probably find we have forgotten the number. It takes a conscious effort to be able to remember the number whenever we need it.

Michie and Johnston (1985) point out that most of our human memory is built up from experience. The DNA molecule in every human cell contains about 1 gigabyte of information, but only a tenth (100 megabytes) of this is accessible. Thus a new-born baby's brain can only start with perhaps a few tens of megabytes to define its initial structure. The rest of its complex structure is built up during a lifetime of experience.

Although the storage capacity of the brain is immense, its speed of processing new information is very modest. We can only take in effectively about 30 bits/second. In a lifetime this might amount to 10 gigabytes. It takes us about 2 seconds to access what is stored in our long-term memory. If I ask you to recall the house where you lived when you were aged 10, you can conjure up that image in about 2 seconds. However, we can only hold a limited number of items at a time in our conscious memory: about seven. We can consciously manipulate information only slowly, compared with an electronic calculator or a computer. However, the brain does have a remarkable facility for discerning pattern in images. When we first encounter an image, we get an impression of its significance very quickly. This is called pre-attentive vision. We may then begin to search more closely and systematically, to understand what we see. Figure 7.4 indicates the immense capacity of raw data in an image, which the brain can assess quickly.

You quickly realize that the image comprises a random pattern of shading, and that the density of the shading decreases (that is, gets lighter) towards the centre of the image. If you had been presented with the same large amount of data numerically, it would have been very difficult for you to discern this simple pattern.

Yet we must be careful. The brain seeks to impose its own understanding of what the senses perceive. This is illustrated in Figure 7.5.

The image comprises six objects. Three are segments of a black disk, and three are bent black lines. Yet the fact that these are rather unusual objects, and that they are arranged in a particular way, convinces the brain that there must be a simpler interpretation of the perceived image. Most people interpret the image as six black disks, and a black line triangle, all overlaid by a white opaque triangle. This illusion is so compelling that you can almost 'see' the edge of the white triangle. The inside of the triangle seems 'whiter' than the

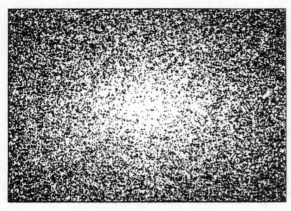

NOTES

This image has 65,772 picture elements, or pixels.

The number of possible images is ten raised to the power 19,799.

Ten thousand million people, each drawing one different image per second for ten thousand million years, would explore less than one seventh of 1% of its capacity.

Figure 7.4   *Image capacity*

Figure 7.5   *Illusion*

outside. Both these impressions are strictly an illusion, but they show the power of the brain in forcing you to interpret data in a way which makes sense in terms of your experience.

What has all this to do with the management use of IT/IS? Well, it raises important issues of how we use people and machines in combination – the *man–machine system*. Both elements have complementary strengths, yet we must ensure that the combination is effective. In any man–machine system you must avoid using the weak features of either (and especially of both!). There are two situations to distinguish: where the man is dominant, and where the machine is dominant.

Where the man is dominant, the systems must be designed to support and help him (or her), rather than to confuse or mislead. Because it is very easy to make computers which process and present data at a rate which far exceeds our human capacity to absorb, this requires a particular discipline on the part of the designer. Moreover the man must have some understanding of what the computer is doing for him, or he will lack confidence in what it delivers. Worse still, he may believe that his own intuition is right, and he will choose to ignore the system. This sometimes happens in vital safety situations, and the results can be potentially disastrous. It happened in the Three Mile Island nuclear power station incident, where an operator did not believe what the computer was telling him to do, and instead did what he instinctively felt was correct in the circumstances. Unfortunately he was wrong.

The second situation is where the machine is dominant. In this case experience has given us enough confidence that the system is more reliable and consistent than the man, or that only the machine is able to act quickly enough to respond to changing circumstances. Thus modern aircraft have 'fly-by-wire' systems which do not directly act upon the instructions given by the pilot through the controls. There is a computer system which intermediates between the pilot and the airframe, taking account of far more factors of safety and aerodynamic performance than any pilot could. We rely on the computer to 'fly' the aircraft, in accordance with general instructions given by the pilot. A second example is the expert system used to control the production of cement (see pages 13–14 and 30–31); there is enough confidence to let the machine control the production process, with only a supervisory and monitoring role for the man.

As a manager, you need to be very clear which category of man–machine system you are putting in:

(a) Information provision systems (or decision support systems) supporting a man who remains in control of the decisions; or
(b) A control system, where the machine takes the detailed decisions, and the man is there mainly to supervize and monitor.

In the first case, the systems must be closely tailored to the needs and limitations of the human user. In the second case the scope of action of the human supervisor must be carefully thought through. If the role is not properly understood, the man–machine system can be ineffective, or even dangerous. The individual needs to know his exact role, and the circumstances in which he would be justified in overruling a machine whose detailed operation he could not judge.

IT and the person

The above discussion was about the detailed level of the man–machine interaction, where issues of perception, memory and human information processing arise. Let's consider the next level: the issues of people's attitude towards IT/IS. We have already addressed this in the context of systems being developed and introduced at work (pages 88–93), but there are wider issues which will affect how we use IT/IS in the future.

Do people just view machines as inanimate objects, or do they in some way 'relate' to them? This is not a trivial question. Many people view their motor cars as almost having a personality, while many men view railway steam engines, for example, as definitely having a personality to which they can relate. It is not just about the detail of the man–machine interaction; it is about our attitude to that interaction.

In the mid-1960s the computer scientist Joseph Weizenbaum developed a system called 'Eliza'. A user could interact with the system through a computer terminal. The system was programmed to maintain a dialogue by simply turning around questions, without any real intelligence or understanding. We can keep a cocktail-party conversation alive in this way simply by making appropriate noises and brief comments to show the other person we are following what they are saying.

It emerged that people got to like their session with Eliza. Indeed they would often be prepared to divulge quite private matters in their dialogue with the machine. This seems to have had some therapeutic value; at least the machine was always (apparently) a sympathetic listener, which is more than most people are! You see a related phenomenon with ATM machines outside banks. Often customers will queue in the rain to use the impersonal but reliable machine rather than go into the bank and deal with the human cashier. It seems important to design systems which behave in a human-like (anthropomorphic) way, so that we can 'understand' them without feeling that they are threatening. Michie and Johnston (1985) have called this the 'human window' for computer systems: we don't want machines which we can't understand or which for any other reason we find threatening.

Individuals will vary in their tolerance of IT/IS. For some, the sight of a VDU or keyboard is an immediate turn-off. For others there is a fascination with the technology and what it can do. Both these extremes are dangerous for the organization. There are some questions which can often show how individuals think on this issue:

- How do you *feel* about IT/IS which you encounter, or have to use?
- Would you *trust* a machine to diagnose your illness and prescribe treatment?
- Would it be *wrong* to hurt a robot which is like a person in appearance?
- Should we ban machines which people can't understand?
- Are computer-generated poetry, music and pictures really 'art'?

Individual attitudes towards IT/IS will often be the underlying limitation, or source of difficulty, when you are tying to use IT fully in your organization. To achieve what you really want, there may be a wider issue of education and persuasion than would at first appear.

IT and the enterprise

Thus the attitudes of individuals directly affect the way in which the enterprise can grow in its use of IT/IS in the future. The broad trends which we have discussed earlier in the book are shown in Figure 7.6.

START DATE	JUSTIFICATION	PURPOSE	MANAGER'S ROLE
1960s	Efficiency	Do the same job better	Cost-cutter
1970s	Effectiveness	Do a better job	Intrapreneur
1980s	Strategic advantage	Better the business	Entrepreneur
1990s	Information enterprise	Build an information-based organization	Infopreneur

Figure 7.6   *Trends in IS*

In the 1990s the benefit and purpose of IT/IS have become broader. They are concerned with strategic advantage and organizational development, rather than with merely automating established business procedures. To create the information-based organization (see page 52), the manager has to adopt the role of 'infopreneur', to be creative and proactive in his use of information as a resource. The infopreneur must develop business procedures supported by IT/IS to survive in the changing business environment. Here are some of the issues which should concern you in your role as infopreneur, and some recent readings which you might wish to examine:

(a) Consider IT/IS as the enabler of organizational development, in an age of continuous change. It has been suggested that the main benefit of IT/IS will be the ability to enable organizations to evolve fast enough to compete and survive. IT/IS becomes part of the fabric of the organization, not something separate and optional. In the terminology of Chapter 5 the IT infrastructure is then a 'must-do' project. See, for example, Butler-Cox (1991).

(b) Look at the examples of best practice in your own or related industries or countries. The quality press has regular reports which you should scan. There are more detailed accounts in the literature: see Wilson (1989) and MSA (1990).

(c) Extend the first of our six guidelines by developing a proactive IS culture within the enterprise, as described by Willcocks (1991).

(d) Understand the relationships between parts of your own organization, and between your organization and other organizations. The senior manager often needs to be mainly concerned with the interrelationships between units which other people manage in detail. See Galliers and Somogyi (1987), Rockart and Short (1989), Henderson (1990), and Konsynski and McFarlan (1990).

(e) Keep a broader vision about how countries compete, and how major enterprises use IT/IS to support their global or international enterprises. See Porter (1990) and Holtham (1989).

(f) Consider how can you combat the increased threat of computer disaster, or deliberate misuse of the information systems on which your organization depends? Issues of data security are well addressed by Cornwall (1987).

The development of the new 'information-based organization' foretold by Drucker may present its own problems and questions:

1   Is it necessary to keep people constantly in touch with their organization, using modern communication systems?

2   If you do, is this acceptable, or even healthy, for the individuals concerned?

3   Are jobs going to be dehumanized, and lacking in any kind of continuity and stability?

4   What are people's expectation of their job, and what is the meaning of a 'career'? Handy (1989) believes that there will be very different answers to these questions in the future. He speaks of the shamrock organization, comprising a professional core of people, services which are contracted-out, and a flexible fringe of workers who come and go.

5   Are telecommuting and the 'electronic cottage' answers to getting and keeping a workforce which will have different expectations and constraints than in the past? Kinsman (1988) addresses these issues.

A recent viewpoint by White (1990) analyses the challenge of information management to organizations in the 1990s. The key features will be flexible corporate structure, global corporate information networks, and a system for managing those networks effectively.

IT and society

As a senior manager, you should be used to taking the wider view of your organization. You must consider its place in the wider physical, business, political, and regulatory environment. You will be aware that there are other 'stakeholders' in your enterprise than the shareholders. Among them are customers, suppliers, employees, society as a whole, pressure groups, the government, international bodies, professional bodies, political parties and even competitors. Issues of corporate responsibility and business ethics now have a higher profile than they did a few years ago, and they impinge on the way the enterprise uses information to support its activities.

At the detailed level there is data protection legislation to safeguard the holding, processing and transfer of data about living, identifiable individuals. There are safeguards against using such data for purposes different from those formally registered. Recently action has been taken against companies which handle credit data about individuals inaccurately, and those who misuse data for purposes of marketing. There is a substantial market in data which can be of value for marketing; it gives rise to concerns about privacy, and business ethics.

At a broader level IT/IS affects whole countries, and the global community as a whole. The electronic mass-media can reach billions of people simultaneously for major world events. The progress of the Gulf War in 1991 is an example of how information can influence, if not dominate, the conduct of international affairs.

It has been estimated that the amount of printed material in the world has doubled every 15 years since the mid-fifteenth century. This amounts to 5 per cent per annum. The total knowledge of humanity (including material held in other than printed form) increases at about 10 per cent per annum. Yet the capacity of information technology is expanding at about 30 per cent per annum, while its cost is falling in real terms at a similar rate. While the technology and its application are growing, there is an increasing polarization between the haves and the have-nots, in respect of 'information' as well as material wealth. Even for the haves there are difficult questions: will only a few citizens be able to make an economic contribution to a society where most of the work is done far more effectively under the control of computers? For the have-nots it is worse. Elmandjra (1986) estimates that on the eve of the twenty-first century:

(a) One tenth of humanity is under-employed or unemployed.
(b) One quarter of humanity is illiterate.
(c) One third of humanity lives below the poverty line.

Information, in the form of education, is perhaps the only way to redress this imbalance.

Taking stock

This chapter has been very much about the 'diverge' mode of management thinking. It is about taking a broader perspective of the future, and the place of IT/IS within it. You need to take such a broader view if you are to lead your organization forward effectively.

To recap, we have taken the historical perspective of 20,000 years of information technology, which teaches us to be cautious about over-enthusiastic hype concerning a new dawn in the affairs of men. Equally, it shows us the accelerating pace of technical development, which produces an increasing opportunity and challenge for us.

We have looked at the way the technology is developing, and seen that there is no limit yet to the rapid expansion we have seen in the last three decades. Indeed with optical technology we can expect an acceleration in the growth in the power of IT. However, there are difficult areas where the power of IT/IS has to be coupled with the power of the human brain. There are important issues of the man–machine system which we are only beginning to understand, and yet which will be crucial if we are to harness the technology effectively. There are issues of individual, collective and societal attitudes towards information systems and the ways in which they are resisted or accepted. Finally, we have seen the broader aspects of information management, which carry such ethical considerations as those associated with other aspects of management.

Some of this may seem remote from the more immediate and pressing business problems you face today. Yet these changes have a habit of creeping up on those who are ill-prepared for them.

Luck, it is said, favours the prepared mind. Make sure your mind is prepared for the future with IT/IS. Figure 7.7 gives the final part of the information management audit.

Guideline: Prepare for the future			
Ser.	Question	Score	Action
1	Do you review your information strategy regularly?		
2	Are you always ready for a diverge-converge discussion about IT/IS?		
3	Have you learnt the historical lessons from the evolution of your IT/IS?		
4	Do you keep abreast of IT developments and opportunities?		
5	Do you have an effective combination of man and machine?		
6	Are you consciously building the new organization?		
7	Are you using IT/IS fully to support that?		
8	Do you have infopreneurs in your organization?		
9	Do you safeguard the information resource of your organization?		
10	Do you use the information resource ethically?		
	TOTALS		

Figure 7.7   *IM audit – Part 6*

The questions all relate to issues addressed in this chapter. More than ever you will need to relate them carefully to the situation of your enterprise. Please answer them critically and honestly. If necessary, look back over the issues discussed in the chapter, and relate them to your situation.

References

Butler-Cox (1991), *The Role of Information Technology in Transforming the Business*, Butler-Cox Foundation, London.
Cornwall, H. (1987), *Data Theft: Computer Fraud, Industrial Espionage and Information Crime*, Heinemann, London.
Elmandjra, J. (1986), 'Learning Needs in a Changing World', *Futures*, Vol. 18, No. 6, pp. 731–7 (Dec.).
Forester, T. (1989), *Computers in the Human Context*, Blackwell.

Galliers, R. D. and Somogyi, E. K. (1987), *Towards Strategic Information Systems*, Abacus Press.

Gosling, W. (1988), 'The Foreseeable Future', *National Electronics Review*, National Electronics Council, London.

Handy, C. (1989), *The Age of Unreason*, Business Books.

Harmon, P. and King, D. (1985), *Expert Systems: Artificial Intelligence in Business*, John Wiley.

Henderson, J. C. (1990), 'Plugging into Strategic Partnerships: the Critical IS Connection', *Sloan Management Review*, Vol. 31, No. 3, pp. 7–18 (Spring).

Holtham, C. (1989), 'Information Technology Management into the 1990s: a Position Paper', *Journal of Information Technology*, Vol. 4, No. 4, pp. 179–96 (Dec.).

Jackson, D. (1981), *The Story of Writing*, Studio Vista, London.

Kinsman, F. (1988), *The Telecommuters*, Wiley, London.

Konsynski, B. R. and McFarlan, F. W. (1990), 'Information Partnerships – Shared Data, Shared Scale', *Harvard Business Review*, Vol. 68, No. 5, pp. 114–20 (Sep.–Oct.).

Michie, D. and Johnston, R. (1985), *The Creative Computer*, Penguin Books, London.

Moravec, H. (1988) *Mind Children*, Harvard University Press.

MSA (1990), 'Excellence and the IT Factor: information technology inside excellent companies in Britain', Management Science America Ltd, in *Journal of Information Technology*, Vol. 5, pp. 41–8 (March).

Oakley, B. (1990), 'The Limits to Growth in IT', *Computing & Control Engineering Journal* (Jan.)

Porter, M. E. (1990), 'The Competitive Advantage of Nations', *Harvard Business Review*, Vol. 68, No. 2, pp. 73–93 (Mar.–Apr.).

Rockart, J. F. and Short, J. E. (1989), 'IT in the 1990s: Managing Organizational Interdependence', *Sloan Management Review*, Vol. 30, No. 2, pp. 7–17 (Jan.).

White, M. (1990), 'Viewpoint', *International Journal of Information Management*, Vol. 10, No. 4, pp. 253–8 (Dec.).

Willcocks, L. (1991), 'Building an Information Systems Culture: How to get There from Here', AMED/AMRG Conference: Individual and Organization Development – Conflict & Synergy (Jan.).

Wilson, T. D. (1989), 'The Implementation of Information System Strategies in UK Companies: Aims and Barriers to Success', *International Journal of Information Management*, Vol. 9, pp. 245–58 (Dec.).

8 Drawing it together: the action plan

Introduction

I hope that in studying the last six chapters you have not lost sight of the structure of the book. This was explained on pages 2–3, and illustrated in Figure 1.1.

This chapter helps you to 'converge' *your* thinking about information management, to produce an action plan which is right for *you* and *your* organization. If you do this carefully, then when you have finished, you should be able to say 'Right. Now I can get on with it'.

The structure of this chapter is simple. Pages 120–122 gives a framework for addressing problems and deciding what to do about them. I would like you to apply this to each of the problem areas which you have identified during the six parts of your information management audit. To help you, pages 122–147 below contain some hints relating to each of the questions you were asked regarding the six guidelines. In most cases the hints refer back to the relevant part of Chapters 2–7. Together, the hints and the cross-references should point a way ahead for each of the problem areas you identified.

The chapter appears to be very long, but please note that the six sets of hints are *not* intended to be read as a continuous piece of text. You should concentrate only on those questions in each part of the audit for which you scored yourself *below* five. This means that you will examine fewer than half the hints in generating your action plan. To look at them ail would be to dissipate your effort, and lose sight of the priorities which are implicit in your audit. Do be selective.

Finally, in this chapter pages 147–148 give some general guidance on implementing your action plan.

Developing the action plan

At the end of each of the last six chapters you were invited to complete the corresponding part of the information management audit. In each case the form for this was the last figure in the chapter. I hope you took time to do that, as a method of reviewing the content of the chapter, and relating the issues to the situation in your business.

However, you may well wish to reconsider some of the issues, now that you have read most of the book, or you may decide you need to repeat the audit more thoroughly, perhaps with the assistance of colleagues. In either case you may find it helpful to use the complete set of forms collected together in *Appendix 1*. They are exactly the same as the earlier forms.

Remember that for each question you should score yourself out of ten, with zero being the worst possible score and ten the best. Be ruthless enough so that the total score for each guideline is somewhere between 25 per cent and 75 per cent. Then identify the questions for which you scored less than five out of ten. These are the problems which you will now concentrate on. If you can't make sense of the questions, then either look back over the relevant chapter or use the hints further on in this chapter.

Having identified the problem areas, you need a systematic approach to constructing an action plan. This is given in Figure 8.1.

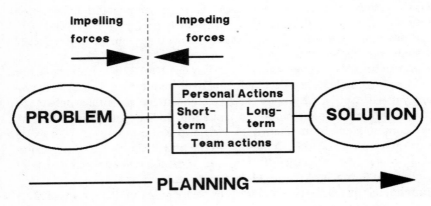

Figure 8.1   *Planning for action*

For each problem, consider carefully what are the:

1   *Impelling forces*: the factors, people or situations which make a solution to the problem easier.
2   *Impeding forces*: the factors, people or situations which make a solution more difficult.

From these, identify:

3   Which *impelling forces* you can take advantage of, in driving towards a solution to the problem.
4   Which *impeding forces* you will need to counter, or avoid, in driving towards a solution.

This process in turn will identify:

5   *Personal actions*, which *you* must take *yourself*. Some of these actions may be wholly yours, but more often your action will be to initiate something to be done by others.
6   *Team actions*, where you will share the action and the responsibility with others. The 'team' might be your senior colleagues, a project team, or any other management grouping appropriate to this purpose.

In each case it will be useful to distinguish between short- and long-term actions.

At this broad level of analysis you can tabulate your conclusions on the forms given in *Appendix 2*. Later you may need to construct a more detailed time–event chart; this is a matter of personal planning, and is beyond the scope of our discussion here.

Let's take a simple example to illustrate the process. Suppose that in Part 1 of your IM audit you decided that Question 2 ('Are Top Managers reluctant to take up IT/IS?') represented a problem in your organization. Perhaps you are a senior manager, immediately below board level, and you know that most board members are reluctant to proceed with IT/IS. You might reason as follows:

The chairman is getting on a bit and doesn't have much idea about IT. He's sharp, though, and might respond if someone he respects presents the case well. The chief executive is better informed about IT/IS, but has never had line responsibility in that area. He's not too sure what to do about IT, either. Both of these people's attitudes are impeding forces, as far as good information management is concerned, and we will need to work on them. My boss, the marketing director, is much more switched on; he has used IT to good effect, and encourages those of us on his staff to do likewise. He's certainly an impelling force for the board in this respect, and I must view him as an ally. In the short term, I need gently to raise with my boss the whole issue of a good information management partnership for our organization, and get him to sow the right seeds with his board colleagues. Then I need to get my team working on the business case for the new marketing database system. By the time that project comes to the board for approval, the climate should be a bit better informed. The boss and I can then pull out the stops with our presentation; he can act as the product champion, making sure the rest of the board are fully with him. That ought to set the climate for a healthier board commitment to what we are doing, and ought to be doing, with IT in our business.

Now think it through for your real-life problem areas, using the hints below.

Hints for guideline 1 – Establish an information management partnership (see Chapter 2)

Is there effective communication between all members of the IM triangle?

The IM triangle was introduced on page 8 and in Figure 2.1. To achieve effective communication between the three parties there needs to be a shared understanding of what information management is, and how the three parties are to make their distinctive contributions. If you lack a shared perception, why is this so? Do you need to develop the thinking of a senior business manager, so that he or she can lead colleagues to a fuller understanding of what information management is all about? Or does the size of the problem mean that you need a more formal method of training, bringing in more people? You may need to call on consultants or training organizations to heighten awareness among senior managers.

Analyse the IM Triangle to decide which player is the more isolated from the other two, and on which side of the triangle communication is weakest. If any one of the three players is relatively isolated, ask yourself who is best placed to influence him/her to improve things. It is easier to influence from the top, where you are underpinned by authority. If top management is the problem, consider who can best exert influence among the top group of managers. If communication is weak on one side of the triangle in particular, consider the organizational measures you can take to correct this. The following questions are also relevant.

Are top managers reluctant to take up IT/IS?

The top manager was considered on pages 9–11. Consider the reason for their reluctance. Is it lack of time, lack of knowledge, or a considered opinion that information management is merely an operational-level topic? Who is best placed to help change that opinion, and can you recruit an ally to sow the right seeds? Can you exert some influence yourself, without appearing too evangelical about the topic?

Consider whether there is an internal, or external, information system which you believe might be of direct value to a senior manager and might be attractive enough to overcome his/her initial reluctance. Experiencing some of the benefits of IT/IS at first hand can encourage people to jump the first hurdle in getting to grips with the subject. Point out the 'leadership' and 'setting an example' aspects of the top managers using the firm's own systems, as well as the direct benefits in improved handling of management information.

Do top managers relate IT/IS to their business thinking?

This takes time. Consider the guidance to top managers given on pages 9–11. Can you, or an ally, set an example by explicitly addressing the 'information' angle of general management discussions? You need gently to dispel the view that IT is something esoteric, out on a limb and only dealt with by specialists. Consider whether there is a 'strategic' use of IT which has proved valuable in the business (or even by a competitor), and which you can use to remind top management that IT/IS can improve the business in ways other than saving money.

You might be able to use the internal mail-circulation system to draw managers' attention to suitably 'strategic' articles about the use of IT/IS, or commission an outsider to give a seminar or run a discussion-meeting, to increase the level of awareness.

Do middle managers/users assess information in product and process?

The middle manager/user was considered on pages 11–16, which also gave examples of 'information' as a resource and the concept of information intensity (Figure 2.2). From your position as a senior manager you can probably influence many of these people as a peer group or as subordinates in the organization. Many of them will tend to focus on operations (the process). Try to broaden their thinking about the process, and also get them to consider the product and how it could be enhanced with IT/IS. Consider whether you, or another suitable catalyst, are well enough informed to inject suitable ideas to stimulate their thinking. If you are in what has historically been a 'commodity' business, you may need to encourage a shift away from viewing it as just producing a commodity, to a view of it offering a 'service'. Why not set up some quality circles, and consider how the customer perceives your business? Encourage market-led thinking rather than production-driven thinking.

Do middle managers/users get a sympathetic response to their needs?

If you cultivate the behaviour recommended on page 16, you can expect the middle manager/users to become more proactive, and thus generate new ideas. Do you have the procedures to make sure that those ideas are given due consideration? This is partly about procedures and partly about attitudes.

If there are procedures, ask yourself whether they are known to those concerned. Ask some users whether they know how to advance their ideas and seek support. You may need to get rid of the 'not invented here' (NIH) syndrome, which tends to squash new ideas. NIH can be shown by IT people and by senior business leaders when confronted with a new idea. Do you have a suggestion scheme which encourages staff at all levels to submit ideas? Do you make sure that successful ideas are rewarded and publicized to others? Consider what happens to ideas which are rejected first time round. Do the proposers feel squashed or encouraged to reformulate them?

Do the senior IT professionals understand the business?

The IT professional was considered on pages 16–18. It is essential that the senior IT people can deal effectively with senior general managers. Have you got the right people and attitudes in place? If not, do you need to develop the existing people with training, or do you need some new appointments?

Ask yourself whether the board has (or could develop) confidence in the top IT person (whether that person is on the board or not). Take account of this if you are recruiting a new person; the top management team will need to play a part in the selection process. Make sure that the senior IT professional has the intellectual capacity, and the interest, to view the business as a whole and to think in business terms.

Do the IT professionals work closely with the users, to apply IT well?

You really need to get the views of users, if possible within the context of recent IT projects. Analyse the reasons for misunderstanding, delay, or shortfall in the functionality of systems actually delivered. Find out whether the users were aware of the procedure used to develop and implement systems; whether they were aware of the contribution they needed to make at the various stages (particularly early and late in the project, and during its operation). Did the users get a clear view of what to expect from the system?

Also check out the IS department, to see what its system development procedures are, what the development backlog is, and whether it is using modern tools effectively by bringing users more closely into the development process. Is the majority of the IS department effort concentrating on developing new systems, or on supporting existing systems and their users? You may need to change the resources to correct this balance.

Consider whether you need to decentralize the IS function, to get IT people alongside the business users more effectively.

Do you have a generic policy for IT/IS, related to the business?

The relationship between the product portfolio and the organization of the IS function was considered on pages 18–21 and in Figure 2.4. You must first decide whether your business is reasonably homogeneous, or whether there is a wide range of type of product or business unit. Then you must ask whether the policy for IT/IS sensibly matches the nature of the business.

If it is a diverse portfolio, then you probably need the full gamut of IT/IS policies, from 'centrally planned' through to 'support'. You may need to educate people, so that they are aware why the policy is not uniform throughout the organization. Consider whether the policy if reviewed often enough, certainly when there is a change in information strategy or when there is an organizational change for other reasons.

Do you have the necessary formal arrangements to control IT/IS?

Besides the issue discussed in the last question, five other organizational aspects were addressed on pages 21–22. Consider, top-down, what your organizational arrangements are for IT/IS, and whether users (general managers) retain the balance of power at each level.

At the top level do you need a steering committee to act as the custodian of the information strategy? The scope of this task needs to be spelt out in terms of reference. At the level of individual projects do you need a joint project team approach or can you rely on the IS department to manage things effectively, in concert with users? You need to consider the enterprise's experience in this respect, and ask whether the lessons from the past have influenced subsequent behaviour. If you feel you are not collectively learning to control IT/IS better, analyse why this is so. Is it because people come and go too frequently, or because project teams disperse too quickly, so that their collective expertise is lost?

Are you growing hybrids in the organization?

Growing 'hybrid managers' (who understand the business and IT/IS equally well) was discussed on page 22. First consider how many people you need to exercise this vital bridging function between IT and general management, at each level. Then consider the people you have in place. Are they acting as hybrids now, do they have the potential to work as hybrids, or are they unlikely to acquire the skills to work as hybrids? The answer to that question should indicate the necessary action clearly enough. It can be better to have a few high-priced individuals who can play the role effectively, rather than a larger number of IT people who will huddle together and not establish a good dialogue with general management.

Training courses are now available to develop hybrid skills, but be careful to clarify the aim. Are you taking IT people and trying to make them better managers of the IS function? Or are you taking IT people and making them into general managers? Or are you taking general managers and adding IT skills to their repertoire?

Hints for guideline 2 – Distinguish the potential benefits of IT/IS (see Chapter 3)

Do you carefully consider all three generic benefits of IT/IS?

The three generic benefits of IT/IS were explained on pages 4 and 27 and in Figure 3.1. If you don't address all three in your organization, this may be due to a problem with the IM partnership (see Guideline 1). It is likely that senior managers, in particular, are taking too narrow (or old-fashioned) a view of the role of IT/IS. Consider who should be doing the broader thinking in your enterprise, and how you can influence or educate them to take a wider view. Often there are just a few key people who need to take a different attitude.

However, there may be a good business reason why you have concentrated on particular generic benefits (usually efficiency). If so, make sure those business reasons are still valid, or do not reflect blinkered management thinking. You may be locked into a view of your business as supplying a commodity, for example, rather than offering a *service* to supply a commodity product.

Do you have some systems which seek mainly efficiency benefits?

Examples of efficiency systems were given on pages 28–31. If you make any use of IT/IS at all, then it is most likely that you started with this category of system. However, there may be opportunities which have passed unnoticed and you need to take a fresh look. Use the classification of management resources given on pages 25–27 to consider what opportunities may have been neglected. Usually such a review requires a critical examination of many of the operational procedures in the organization. Who is best placed to do this, and how can you initiate studies of operational matters without incurring mistrust or suspicion? You may need to work on the hearts and minds of middle and operational managers to get the necessary climate of support. You might be able to use quality circles, to get work teams to take collective responsibility for examining this issue and coming up with ideas for improvement. Because efficiency benefits are the most tangible, operational staff often find them easier to understand than other benefits, and to formulate ideas accordingly.

Can you identify those benefits, and the cost savings?

Look back at the business cases which were made, and approved for the efficiency systems which you now have in place. Did they identify the benefits, and does anyone now make sure they are being achieved? If this has been overlooked or forgotten (as commonly happens), is it worth introducing a monitoring system or undertaking an audit? For an existing system, only do so if there is likely to be a useful lesson to learn. It is important to learn the lessons from these past experiences, and to resolve to put procedures in place to manage benefits better in the future, in accordance with Guideline 5.

If the benefits were monitored, did the original estimates of savings prove realistic or not? Try to sense whether people were being deliberately over-ambitious because that was the only way to get their pet project approved, or whether there was some genuine misunderstanding about the business process and what the information system could do. If the latter, ask yourself whether you would have a better understanding of the business now, as a basis for the business case.

Do you have some systems which seek mainly effectiveness benefits?

Examples of effectiveness systems were given on pages 31–35. If you are fairly advanced in your use of IT/IS, it is most likely that systems you are now implementing, or have recently implemented, are in this generic category. Therefore consider whether you have an adequate system for:

(a) *Looking for opportunites.* Do you rely on users to shout? Have you considered all the categories of management resource listed on pages 25–27 and used on pages 31–35?
(b) *Prioritizing projects.* Do you say yes to the user who shouts loudest, or do you manage to weigh the risk and return of IT investments?

Because effectiveness systems now impact upon the middle and senior levels of the organization, are enough people at those levels giving it active consideration? Consider whether there is subconscious or deliberate resistance to addressing the issues, for fear of the consequences.

Can you identify those benefits, and the increased return on assets?

Examine the business case which was made, and approved, for recent and current projects. Are the benefits being monitored and reported back to senior management? In looking at each case are *you* convinced that the benefits are being achieved? If not, who *is* being convinced, and is it on slim evidence? Consider whether your procedures for approval and monitoring need review.

Have you got a clear collective view of what 'return on assets' means for the various management resources? For energy, it should be clearly quantified. For people, it is more difficult; you may need to rely on a subjective assessment of the 'return on management' for individuals. If so, make sure that those same individuals are asked to reassess the situation regularly and give their honest view as to whether their effectiveness has indeed been improved by the system.

Do you have some systems which seek mainly strategic advantage (edge)?

Examples of systems for strategic advantage were given on pages 35–40. Many organizations have not yet started to introduce strategic (or competitive edge) systems, but those that do can get a considerable advantage from them. If you don't have any yet, ask whether this is because the management thinking is too narrow. If so, does the fault lie with senior management? Guideline 1 is relevant to this.

Consider the four classes of strategic system given on page 35, and ask yourself whether there are opportunities in your area of business. If you do have some strategic systems, ask whether they had a product champion at senior level. If some systems failed, was this due to lack of a champion or for some other reason from which you can learn a lesson?

Can you identify those benefits, and the resulting business growth?

Find out whether the strategic systems which you have were driven by senior management, and hence bypassed the normal approval procedures required of other projects. In any case, were the benefits thought through carefully, and has the subsequent business performance been monitored? It should be businessmen and users who decide whether the system has achieved the planned benefits, not IT professionals. Perhaps you need to tighten up the approval procedures, so that the business benefits can be identified and then monitored consistently?

Check whether it is evident that the business-performance measure being used is really likely to be influenced by the system concerned. Then, if there does seem to have been an improvement in business performance, can you be sure it was due to the system? Perhaps someone was trying to kid you (or themselves). If there is serious doubt in this area, are users and management jointly trying to assess the position honestly, or are there entrenched positions (perhaps based upon who was the sponsor of the project, and therefore has a personal interest in its success)? Problems of this kind are symptoms of a failure to jointly 'own' the system at the approval stage.

Can you provide the right management framework for different benefits?

The broader management framework is the subject of Guideline 1. Here you should be concerned with your ability to deal with all three generic benefits of IT/IS, in terms of formulating proposals, approving projects, and then managing them through to operation. Pages 40–42 gave an overview of the case-studies discussed in Chapter 3, and the classification framework for using IT/IS. Ask yourself whether the procedures, and method of thinking in your organization would be able to identify each of these types of opportunity, recognize the differences, and manage each of them appropriately. Do the examples have parallels with what you are doing? If not, are you missing an opportunity and do you need to develop new procedures or allocate a more senior level of responsibility for taking an overview of this matter?

Can you cope with differences between planned and actual benefits?

We mentioned on page 41 how the real benefits of many systems evolve; systems put in for one purpose can actually deliver benefits in unexpected directions. It is better to plan ahead (or at least to monitor and adjust) the management use to which you put systems. Thus an efficiency system can sometimes be developed to enhance effectiveness or strategic benefits. Ideally you should do this in a controlled way, but for most organizations it has been largely unplanned. Remember that it is better to have a monitoring system and discover the unexpected, than to have no monitoring system at all. See whether you have put an adequate monitoring system in place for new systems. What do you do if things turn out differently than the plan suggested? Do your people believe you would examine this situation constructively (by honest and open-minded review of the situation), or negatively (by criticizing their performance or their judgement in making the original estimates)? Their answer to that question could influence the extent to which they tell you the facts.

Do you have an integrated portfolio for IT/IS?

This was discussed on pages 41–42, with Figure 3.3. If you do not have an integrated portfolio, addressing all the categories summarized in Figures 3.2 and 3.3, then ask yourself why.

The integrated portfolio approach needs a conscious decision whether to reap all the benefits of efficiency systems as savings, or to 'invest' some of the savings in effectiveness systems. Similarly higher internal effectiveness (improving return on assets) can lead to strategic advantage by enhancing external effectiveness.

Perhaps there is a need for education of senior managers, or perhaps they need a methodology, such as the one given in this book, to help them address the issues systematically? Perhaps there is good reason why, in your business or industry, not all the categories are appropriate? If so, make sure that this is a conscious decision rather than one made by neglect or from a position of ignorance.

Hints for guideline 3 – Think strategically about information management (see Chapter 4)

Do you have senior managers using strategic cognitive skills?

The strategic skills of senior managers were discussed on pages 44–48. Consider whether you have enough senior people (including yourself) who have the ability to plan with a 5-year timescale. Are they passive or active about shaping the future for your organization? Are they able to take the 'helicopter view' of it? Have they the vision to 'plan the voyage' ahead? If you think your top managers are weak in this respect, ask whether it is because of a limitation of ability (in which case you need new blood), or because they are simply bogged down by the pressures of routine management and 'firefighting' operations. If the latter, then ask whether your allocation of duties, and organizational structure, give enough time for top management to get to grips with strategic issues. Do you have, or need, a separate strategic planning function? If so, you need an internal communication system to keep it in step with the thinking of top management, so that it does not lose the reality of what happens in the business now.

Do you use the three-step creative approach to vision and strategy?

Pages 48–50 discussed the three-step approach to strategic planning. There are other and more detailed methodologies, but they must include the creation of the vision as a discrete act; this is what makes strategic planning different from detailed business planning. Is the approach used in your organization well understood by the planners, and is the process visible enough to those who are not planners? If not, you may not be laying the right foundations for subsequent communication of the vision and implementation of the strategy.

Ask whether you need to take more steps to encourage brainstorming, and the collective act of lateral thinking. You might consider strategic planning courses or weekend retreats to help with this. Often it is necessary to give senior management a stimulus, away from the immediate pressures of the organization, to remove blinkers from their thinking. It may be necessary to build up their team working, initially in day-to-day matters but gradually extending it to more strategic tasks.

Do you recognize the 'information' aspect of the challenge to managers?

The challenge to managers and the 'information' aspect of it, were addressed on pages 50–52. Are those issues debated among your top managers, formally or informally? Do you need to set time aside, perhaps with a seminar, teach-in or brainstorming session, to take this occasional view of how the world out there is changing? This relates to the last question.

Ask whether the shift towards Drucker's 'knowledge-based organization' makes sense in the context of your enterprise. Identify for yourself how the organizational pyramid can become flatter if supported by better information handling; how you need to respond to expected shortages of skilled staff; whether you can build stronger links with your suppliers, customers and other outside bodies; and how you can 'informate' the processes in your enterprise, rather than automate the historical command-and-control model of management. Use the checklist of these and other issues in Figure 4.7 to see whether your thinking is broad enough.

Have you considered the internal view of strategy enough?

The internal view, based on the value chain, was discussed on pages 52–54 and Figure 4.8. It is just one way of making sure that you systematically review all the internal activities (primary and secondary) of the process by which you produce your good or service for the market. The precise approach does not matter, but ask yourself whether in fact you undertake a thorough internal review.

If all is not well, perhaps you should get a study under way? If you do, make sure it is not dominated by operational people who are locked into the way they do things now. If the study is to be strategic, then there has to be an element of creative lateral thinking about how things could be done differently. You may need to look at other related industries, or at the current practice elsewhere in your industry, to get new ideas. You may need some consultancy support, to bring independent views and questions.

Have you considered the external view of strategy enough?

This is an area of concern for the senior manager, at least in terms of business policy. It was discussed on pages 54–57, where the five-force industry model, sector analysis, and the external value chain were suggested as tools to aid senior managers' thinking in this area. Ask yourself whether your top management team addresses the issue at all, and if so whether its members use these or other suitable tools to do so. Do they need some training, or can you personally take a lead in getting the issues addressed?

Are you in the habit of considering what your enterprise looks like from the customer's viewpoint? Have you asked your customers recently what they think about you, and how your service to them could be improved? Get yourself into the mind-set of the customer, and then ask yourself:

(a) How can I surprise my customer (by giving him what he doesn't normally expect)?
(b) How can I delight my customer (by giving him what he hasn't ever expected before)?

Whatever the management procedure by which you conduct this debate, make sure you end up with a clear view of your competitive position, what your generic business strategy is, how you can target a strategic initiative, and how you can use IT/IS to support that initiative. These are big issues, and you may need to tread carefully if you are not yourself a member of the top management team.

Have you considered the dynamic view of strategy enough?

We considered this on pages 57–63, where the benefit-level matrix (BLM) was introduced as a tool for tracing the evolution in the role of IT/IS in your business and in the industry as a whole (especially your competitors). The important question is whether you have a clear corporate view of the evolution of the use of IT/IS in both these respects.

Ask yourself who in the organization is looking at this in detail, and how is it being addressed by top management as a whole? Do you need to enhance someone's terms of reference to make sure it is done? Make sure that whichever tool is used to analyse the evolution, it is sensitive enough for you to ascribe dates to the various stages. It is fairly easy to identify the broad trends, but you need a more detailed knowledge of the industry to predict the timing of developments. Remember the saying that people tend to over-estimate what will happen in 5 years, and under-estimate what will happen in 10 years.

Can you use the benefit-level matrix to plot the evolution of your IT/IS?

This question and the next one are the detailed aspects relating to the last question. Understanding the current situation (in your organization and in its industry as a whole) is a necessary prelude to planning ahead. The use of the BLM for this was discussed on pages 57–63. Whatever method you use, are you able to see how systems have evolved in the past? Does it make evident how competitive edge is eroded when successful systems become the industry norm? Are you able to estimate the timescale for this? As mentioned for the last question, you may need to task some individual or group to take this historical look at the evolution of IT/IS.

Can you use the BLM to plan ahead, for the industry and your enterprise?

Based on this analysis of the past, you should be able to plan ahead, in the way indicated on pages 57–63. You need first to discern, or estimate, the industry trends and what technology is likely to make possible. Then you need to make a conscious choice as to whether, in respect of the application of IT/IS, you will be a 'leader' (with higher risk, but high potential business reward) or a 'follower' (with lower risk, but no source of competitive edge).

Both decisions can be right, for some organizations, but indecision is indefensible! You need to weigh how important IT/IS will be in your business strategy. It may be the central plank (as in many strategies within the finance industry), or it may be peripheral. However, if you are intent on getting competitive edge from IT/IS, then make sure you are planning your 'encore', to keep ahead of the competition. If you aren't, is there a mistaken view prevalent that 'competitive use of IT/IS' is a one-off recipe for lasting business success?

Do you have an information strategy closely linked to business strategy?

The information strategy provides a formal 'peg in the ground', recording the outcome of your strategic deliberations. It should establish a framework for the detailed use of IT/IS in the organization. You should have a corporate business strategy, supported in turn by an information strategy (as well as strategies for other aspects of management, such as human-resources management).

The information strategy was discussed on pages 63–66 and in Figure 4.15. Check whether all the parts of that figure are being dealt with adequately. Does the logic flow from business aims, to people, to technology? Is there adequate consideration of historical constraints, and policy for the future regarding such issues as standards? Ask yourself who has the responsibility for developing the information strategy (perhaps the IS department), and who has the responsibility for approving and policing it (perhaps a user-run steering committee)?

Does the information strategy cover business, functionality, and IT/IS?

This relates to the last question, and was dealt with on page 65. Consider whether the scope and detail of the information strategy is appropriate to the organizational structure of your enterprise. If you are a conglomerate, then you may need a 'minimalist' corporate information strategy. If your business is fairly homogeneous, then you may need a strong and fairly uniform policy from the centre.

The three related aspects of the strategy should provide the link between users and IT professionals. Ask yourself whether this is so, or whether one partner has been dominant in the definition of the strategy. If so, then you may need to correct the power balance in the handling of IS matters.

Hints for guideline 4 – Identify the benefits, and their value (see Chapter 5)

Is the information strategy a 'peg in the ground' for IS planning?

This relates to the last question but one. The information strategy should provide a record of senior management's strategic discussion, *and* be widely available to those who need to use and interpret it for planning individual systems. For both reasons it should be formally documented. Check what the situation is for your own organization. It may be that it has not been properly recorded, is not regularly reviewed, or is not widely enough disseminated.

Check too on the arrangements for monitoring that the strategy is in fact complied with. The IS department will have the major responsibility in respect of the technical aspects of the strategy, but business and general managers will have the responsibility for the successful business use of the information which is handled by the systems. Usually a steering committee, with users in the chair (or majority), is the senior forum with responsibility for the information strategy formulation and policing. The board is of course responsible for endorsing it formally.

Does senior management oversee the 'convergence' process of planning?

See page 68. The information strategy is the turning point from the 'divergence' of strategic discussion to the 'convergence' on to detailed planning and implementation of systems. The senior management naturally has the main responsibility for the first, but also needs to keep a management overview of the second. Chapters 5 and 6 are about the process of convergence.

Ask yourself whether the senior management in your enterprise distinguishes these two aspects clearly, and discharges both sets of responsibilities effectively. It is not uncommon for the balance to be quite wrong. If so, you may need to educate senior management to correct matters.

Do you justify various types of IS according to a consistent set of rules?

Look at the systems which have been approved recently in your organization, and determine the formal process to which they were subjected. Is there a well-defined procedure, and if so, is it applied consistently? Ask whether senior management ever short-circuits the procedures applied to other projects, and why this might be. Pages 68–70 suggest possible reasons.

There may be a culture conflict in the organization, between those who believe that the financially-hard case should be the only type recognized, and those who believe that softer benefits must be recognized. Is this polarization a dangerous one in your organization?

Do you recognize, and deal with, the 'must-do' category of IS?

This was discussed on page 70, and the survey (Figure 5.2) showed that about half of all organizations experience this category in practice. Therefore consider what might constitute a must-do project in the context of your business. It might be something imposed from outside, by a regulatory body or even a dominant trading partner; or it might be the result of evolving industry standards for electronic transactions, which you can't afford to ignore. Look at existing systems, and see if any were handled differently because they were must-do systems.

Then consider how you *ought* to deal with that category. The basic principle is that you should not waste time and effort making an elaborate business case. However, this does not remove the need to meet the requirement efficiently. This will often be a detailed technical matter for the IS department, and is separate from the confirmation of the must-do nature of the requirement (which is a business decision).

Do you recognize a range of types of business case for IS?

The six 'milestones' for sharpening up the business case were discussed on pages 70–71. Take an audit of the way the business case was made for recently approved systems in your organization, to see whether the type of business case reflected the range of types of benefit, from hard to soft. If there is not enough tangible evidence, then discuss the issue with the appropriate people (individually) to see whether there is a consensus of opinion or a well-defined procedure. Check whether there is evidence of the polarization of practice between acts of faith, on the one hand, and hard financial cases, on the other.

If all is not well, then the issue needs to be addressed at least at IS steering committee level, to formulate appropriate guidance. This body will then be responsible for seeing that the guidance is followed, and that the business case is sharpened as far as possible, thus laying the foundation for the subsequent management of the benefits (see Guideline 5).

Are numbers used unrealistically, in trying to quantify benefits?

The last question is about whether a procedure exists; this question is about whether it is adequate in detail. There are two ways you might explore this issue:

(a) Ask those who have been required to make the business case for recent projects whether they were really comfortable with the extent to which they had been required to quantify the detail. Were they producing numbers, because they knew that only numbers were acceptable? Were they extravagant in their claims, because they knew this was the only way the project would be approved?
(b) Check whether the detail of the business case led immediately to the definition of objective, quantified measures of the impact of the system which could be used to monitor subsequent operational success.

If either of these approaches shows a weakness, then you need a wider study to formulate better procedures. Make full use of the experience gleaned so far.

Could you sharpen up the way you make the business case?

This relates to the last two questions, and to the discussion on pages 68–72. Compare the practice in your organization to the practice reported in the survey of managers. Consider the tentative conclusions from that survey, and how your organization could improve.

An important issue is often the role of the accountants in the approval process. They will almost inevitably press for the most financially based case that is possible. By controlling their level of influence, you may therefore be able to control the flavour of the business cases which succeed. It can be the case that they are relatively over-influential for smaller projects, and under-influential for larger projects (which can be pushed through by senior management, bypassing normal procedures).

Is your investment culture the same for IS as for other resources?

This important issue was discussed on pages 78–81. The question can only be answered by the top management team, which will probably have to think very carefully about it. It is possible that IT/IS investment proposals are dealt with more rigorously than, less rigorously than, or equally rigorously as, proposals for other types of investment. If there is no consistency, ask whether this is right. It might be right, but the presumption must be that all investment proposals should be judged by similar criteria. Speak with the sponsors for other types of investment, to find out how they were required to justify the proposals. Their practical experience may differ from the 'policy' answer you receive from top management.

Do you 'package' proposals, in order to match the investment culture?

Packaging of proposals was discussed on pages 79–80. It is a matter of matching the proposals and the related business case to the investment culture of the organization. There is nothing inherently wrong with this unless people are being compelled to present things they cannot wholly believe in. This relates to the question opposite.

Sometimes the investment culture is so harsh that only *bona-fide* cost-saving systems survive. If this is so, then ask whether the business situation warrants it (the 'necessary evil' generic policy for IT/IS), or whether it is likely that real opportunities for other benefits are thereby being denied to the organization.

Do you consciously balance risk and return, for IS investment?

This issue was discussed on pages 80–81. Like the last question but one, this is an issue for top management, which may judge proposals *ad hoc*, or may choose a portfolio approach which consciously looks for a balance of risk and return. Get the perspective of the financial planning staff in the organization, to see whether the policy is actually reflected in practice. It may be that management keeps very quiet about this issue, not wishing to encourage highly speculative proposals from lower levels of the organization. This may be fair, but you should at least ask whether this is a consistent way to behave, and whether the implicit assumption (that only top management can conceive a viable high-risk high-return project) is in fact well-founded.

Hints for guideline 5 – Manage the achievement of the benefits (see Chapter 6)

Do you manage information systems as people, procedures, and technology?

This is about taking the broad view of what an 'information system' comprises. In the business context it embraces people, procedures and technology. This was discussed on pages 83–85. Some people will take a narrower view, to include just the technology, but as a senior manager it is important that you redress the balance. The technology will only be beneficial if it is supporting or enabling 'good' business procedures which will lead to an identifiable business benefit.

You should insist on this broad perspective during the formulation of the information strategy. Here, a similar principle should be applied during the design and implementation of individual IT/IS projects. Consider people first, then the procedures they will use, then the technology which supports them in this. If your organization is not taking this perspective, then ask where the thinking needs to be broadened. Consider whether you have sufficient influence to get such a change of thinking, remembering that 'authority' and 'influence' are not the same thing. You may need to work on a few key individuals, particularly those concerned with the progression of projects, such as members of the IS steering committee and individual project teams.

Do you give the right balance of management attention to these three?

This relates to the last question above, and to pages 83–85. There is often a tendency for project managers to concentrate on the visible project – the hardware and software. This is quite natural: their terms of reference, their performance and their credibility are all tied up with the success of the named project. You must of course encourage a wider view, from all people engaged in IT/IS projects. However, the reality is that you will probably need to correct the balance of attention towards the benefit and people aspects. This can be reflected in the questions you ask as a senior manager. The message will soon get around that you insist on taking the broad, business-oriented perspective of the project and will not be satisfied with any narrower view of it. With your peers at senior level, you will need to present a balanced view, while encouraging others (such as senior human-resource management staff) to take responsibility as well as merely an interest in what is going on. Team commitment at senior level, nurtured by a product champion, is a powerful recipe for success.

Do you know the project life-cycle, or equivalent, used in your business?

You need a broad awareness of the system development procedure used by your IS department (or by your consultants/contractors if you are using them). Make sure you understand its principles, and make sure that it includes the essential features of bridging between IT professionals and eventual users. These were described on pages 85–88, with an example of a six-phase project life-cycle.

You should ask your IT professionals why they use a particular approach. Is it widely proven elsewhere? Is it known to be appropriate to your business sector, or type of enterprise? Is it a proprietary approach, and, if so, does it tend to lead you into the direction of solutions offered by a particular vendor?

Consider the extent to which the procedure allows you to retain competition in the work. If you want the maximum scope for competition, e.g. with a very large project, you can separate the feasibility study, the detailed requirements analysis, design and production, and operational support. Each of these can be the subject of competitive tendering; this is slower and more expensive initially, but may be worth it to make sure you have got a major investment right.

Do you consciously adapt the project life-cycle for urgent or complex cases?

This relates to the last question, and to the discussion on pages 87–88. Just as you can adapt the project life-cycle to maximize competition by suppliers, so you can adjust it to speed up the development process, or deal with a complex or uncertain user requirement. Look at examples of recent projects in your organization, and ask whether the procedure was adapted to special circumstances or not. The ideal is probably to have a flexible interpretation of one basic approach, so that the principles are well understood but the detail will vary from project to project.

Consider also the duration of the project. If it is likely to be lengthy, then piloting/prototyping can be a method of maintaining user awareness and enthusiasm, as well as serving the more immediate purpose of gaining confidence that the user's requirement has been correctly interpreted.

If the procedure is adapted, then of course the senior management team will need to be quite clear what plan it is judging progress against.

Do you know what threats your people perceive from IT/IS?

Pages 88–90 and Figure 6.3 identified six types of concern or fear which people may have about IT/IS and its impact on their working lives. As a manager, you are probably robust enough to have overcome, or successfully avoided, many of these fears yourself. This is dangerous, because it means you may not fully understand the apprehensions of others. Try to think yourself into their situation, and consider the view *they* have of the systems you are planning. Has anyone told them how the systems will directly affect them, and tried to discuss their concerns with them? The quotations given on pages 89–90 put some realism into the way people really think about IT/IS.

When you have thought about this yourself, ask your managers and IT professionals whether they *know* what the undercurrents are in the organization. Has there been any informal discussion, and what messages come across from the questions asked (or not asked) at any consultative meetings you may have held?

Finally, walk the floor yourself, and find out how people are thinking and, more important, how they are *feeling* about IS projects. Don't be afraid of using the question 'How do you feel about this project?' People have hearts as well as minds.

Do you take appropriate action at the right time in the project life-cycle?

Pages 91–93 and the lower part of Figure 6.3 indicated what you need to do to allay people's fears about IT/IS (or indeed about most other things). They sound fairly obvious, but ask yourself first whether they are really done properly in your organization.

Then ask yourself whether you are getting the timing right, in relation to the life-cycle of the project itself. If the users will perceive a lengthy hiatus in a major project, then this can be a factor in deciding whether to have a pilot/prototype project (see the last question but one). Re-exposure to the project, and direct participation at what is now a more tangible and exciting phase, can be a strong motivator.

Keeping the project and people aspects in step can be a problem. Even a few days can be critical, if people have been trained to use the system, and then it is delayed and they are sitting around waiting for it. As a senior manager, you need to watch both sets of milestones carefully.

Finally, be watchful of the characteristic four stages of implementing change. Be ready for the middle two stages, where you may need to give extra leadership and encouragement from your level, to maintain faith in the project.

Do you consciously practise benefit management for IT/IS?

The principles of this were discussed on pages 93–97. If you have established the right information partnership (see Guideline 1). constructed your inform-ation strategy correctly (see Guideline 3), and identified requirements as part of the project life-cycle (see first question on page 139), then this should be relatively simple. There will be a clear framework of understanding, from which you can integrate the management of the benefits into the normal management arrangements.

However, if things have been less than perfect, then you will have to take some corrective action. This should be as urgent and specific as the success of the particular project demands. You should consider a formal review of the user requirement (so that it is justified in business terms, with identifiable benefits); a review of the numbers, levels, and types of appointment of the people to be served by the system; a change in the monitoring arrangements, so that there is some measure of performance; or a retrospective review (audit) of the whole system, with an open mind about its retention. None of these measures is likely to be popular or comfortable, but weigh them against the risk of continuing with an expensive system with uncertain benefits. However, do not neglect the more general lessons which should be applied in future: make sure you have a procedure which integrates benefit management in the way described in the next three questions.

Are requirements and benefits defined and agreed together, by users?

See pages 94–95 and the third column of Figure 6.4. It is vitally important that benefits and requirements are identified together. If you are weak on this, then set the principles to be adopted in the future. For a small, quick project the procedure is quite simple to apply. For a larger and more complex project you may need to consider:

(a) Whether there are many users of a similar type, who should be treated as a group for the purposes of deciding benefits and requirements. If so, a suitable forum will be needed, where the users feel that they are retaining control.
(b) If the timescale of the project is such that people are likely to have moved to other jobs, make sure that the deliberations are documented, so that successors can at least understand the business rationale for what they are being given (and the responsibility they are being invited to accept).
(c) If the timescale of the project is such that the business situation is likely to change during the design and implementation of the project, then make sure there is a mechanism for revising requirements. This *must* be done in a

highly controlled way, or it encourages afterthoughts, wish-lists, changes of heart, and other recipes for disorder.

Is the achievement of the benefits monitored, in subsequent operation?

See pages 93–95 and the third column of Figure 6.4. The 'contract' between the user and the provider of IT/IS offers business benefit in exchange for system functionality. This contract must be the basis for the management procedures which monitor the operational performance of the system in the wider sense. Thus individuals' objectives should reflect those benefits once the system comes into operation.

This principle is simple, but can be organizationally difficult. It comprises a handover from those who are engaged with the project to those who are concerned with routine line management. Achieving a smooth handover is one argument for not having two entirely separate groups of people for each purpose. A particular danger is that the project team disperses once a system comes into operation, and loses its collective expertise. Consider those who are likely to be key link-men, or need to remain available to give suitable support to the users.

Does senior management monitor progress, or have witch-hunts afterwards?

See pages 93–95, and the comments at the top of page 141. Because senior managers are so much concerned with change, rather than routine operations, it is easy for them to neglect the progress of implementing projects and their subsequent operation. There needs to be a mechanism by which the project team, or the steering committee which oversees it, reports regularly to top management. The format should balance the project, people, and benefit aspects. The procedure should be followed until the system is well into operation, and enough evidence has been built up to confirm that the business benefit has in fact accrued. If the benefit does not accrue, there is then a management mechanism in place to look more closely at the situation.

There may be an entirely valid reason for failure: the business situation may have changed, competitors may have taken actions which have upset our plans, or a deliberate high-risk venture may simply have collapsed. The question you should ask yourself as a senior manager is whether the situation was being monitored closely enough, and whether the problems should reasonably have been foreseen. At all costs, avoid an adversarial situation while determining the facts of the case. The time may come for reprimand (or even disciplinary action), but that situation should be the product of a controlled management review, not a hasty or ill-tempered one.

Hints for guideline 6 – Prepare for the future (see Chapter 7)

Do you review your information strategy regularly?

The information strategy was introduced on pages 63–66, where it was suggested that it should take a 5-year view but be regularly reviewed, perhaps every 12–18 months. The principles of this were recalled on page 100. The important points are that the information strategy should offer a stable framework for the development and evolution of information systems, but it should itself evolve to reflect changes in the business environment or in the opportunities of new technology.

This is a difficult balance to strike. At one extreme is the view that formulating the strategy is a once-for-all activity. This view is too narrow, and needs changing. The time-horizon of the strategy and the frequency of its review may be indicated by plotting the evolution of systems in your business, or industry, on the benefit-level matrix, as described on pages 57–63. If competitive-edge systems become the industry norm within 2 years, you probably need to take a shorter view than 5 years, and review information strategy more frequently than annually.

Are you always ready for a diverge–converge discussion about IT/IS?

The diverge–converge model of management discussion was described on page 68, while on pages 99–100 we suggested that you should be ready to repeat the cycle. You should do this not only on the occasion of a regular review of the information strategy (see the last question) but also when some new challenge, opportunity or idea becomes evident.

As a senior manager, you need to cultivate this proactive style, in information management as in other aspects of the business activity. You need 'ideas' people, and you need a culture which is receptive to ideas and will give them serious consideration. A suggestion scheme, and active support and encouragement from senior level, can help stimulate the right attitude. The senior manager who sweeps aside discussions of the 'information' aspects of the business is likely to limit the scope of thinking to strictly operational matters.

Have you learnt the historical lessons from the evolution of your IT/IS?

The long history of IT was described briefly on pages 100–103. Find someone who can give you the long, historical view of the evolution of IT/IS in the business. Make sure you get the facts, and separate them from the opinion. Often those with the longest personal knowledge of the systems are those have got into a rut, and therefore they may be poorly placed to give you advice about future development.

Piece together the history, and the reasons why key decisions were made. You may learn much about the culture of the organization, the way information management has been handled, and the attitudes of key people. Then judge whether the culture and the people have changed, so that the climate is different. Try to decide whether your enterprise has been a leader or follower in the industry, whether that position was consciously chosen, and whether a different policy might now be appropriate.

Look also for disaster stories. If there were projects which were late, were over budget, or which under-performed, then ask why this was so. Consider whether, as a springboard for future development, you need to get extra IT advice or resources, adopt more rigorous procedures, or bring the IT professionals closer to the business users.

Do you keep abreast of IT developments and opportunities?

Pages 103–108 dealt with future trends in IT. Consider some of the developments, and what opportunity they might offer to your enterprise: knowledge-based systems (including expert systems), flexible database technology, optical-storage systems, high-capacity telecommunication links and networks, cheaper processing power and smaller computers.

As a senior manager, you need to keep a general awareness of the developments in IT. Watch the appropriate pages in the quality press, particularly those which describe applications in your industry or a related one. Make sure your staff take a similar interest, by raising the issues in casual conversation and by circulating appropriate journals. But don't expect general managers to absorb technical publications; they are for the IT professionals.

Instead use consumer-oriented publications such as *What to Buy for Business*, or abstracting services such as *Business Automation*, which index the abstracts according to the application area (such as health, finance, education). It is easier for managers to relate to such descriptions, than be expected to assess IT from cold technical detail.

Do you have an effective combination of man and machine?

The man–machine system was considered on pages 108–113. Your view of a business information system as a combination of people, procedures and technology almost obliges you to consider the man–machine system as a whole. But you need to pay particular attention to it when the total system has to operate in real-time (so that it is not possible to 'stop and think'), where safety is important, or where complex systems are being controlled.

Can you identify such applications in your business? Ask yourself whether the man–machine aspects were considered by those who designed the systems, and are still understood by those who use the systems. Sometimes there is a lack of communication between the designers and the users. You may get useful information by chatting to people who 'monitor' the operation of machines. Do they really know what situations they are looking for, what they would do if those situations arose, and how they will know that their judgement deserves to overrule the machine?

Are you consciously building the new organization?

The role of IT/IS in the evolution of the organization was discussed on pages 113–115. Do you, and your senior colleagues, have a view of what your organization will look like in 5 years' time? And in 10 years' time? Are you likely to follow the widely forecast trends of flatter management structures, more flexible workforces, a greater emphasis on taking responsibility in groups, and reward for results? Or do you believe it is different in your business, industry, location or culture? Without doubt those around you will be using 'information' as a more powerful tool than before; you need to have a place in that new order or you are likely to be out of business.

Whatever your long-term vision of the organization, are you able to prepare others for the changes? You need to decide whether the steps should be small and often, or large and less frequent. There is a view that all change is costly, so it is better to make bold, major changes rather than keep making minor changes. Which is right for your organization? If these questions have not been asked, or not recently answered, then you may need to work on your senior colleagues to open the debate.

Are you using IT/IS fully to support that?

This relates to the last question. When those general questions have been answered, then the place of IT/IS in making the change possible should become clear. An electronic office system can be a first step in encouraging new lines of communication and 'networking', to loosen the hold of established procedures. Giving PCs to those who have not had them before can open their minds to the opportunities of how different things might be.

There is a second angle to consider. This is the possible role of IT/IS as the enabler, rather than just the supporter, of organizational change. Relate this to page 144, where we suggested that when you become aware of technical advances, you should judge them in terms of the opportunity they present for your business. Consider the enabling applications such as:

(a) Teleworking, to open up a wider and more flexible workforce.
(b) The use of knowledge-based systems to capture the experience of those about to retire, or those whose knowledge could be more valuable if it were more widely available in the organization.
(c) Decentralizing or dispersing your business, while maintaining electronic rather than physical links.
(d) Providing the information for work teams to act more independently, and be more conscious of the quality and other consequences of what they do.

Do you have 'infopreneurs' in your organization?

The term 'infopreneur' was coined on pages 113–114 to describe a manager who is proactive in the use of IT/IS in support of the business. He or she is entrepreneurial by nature, but has the 'information' dimension in mind throughout. Ask yourself whether there is anyone in your organization who fits this description. If not, then why not?

If you are in an information-intensive business, then infopreneurs may be the only people who can assure its future. Take the issue seriously. There are two steps you might consider to improve things:

(a) Cultivate 'hybrids' who know the technology and the business (see page 22), then groom these people through management posts to a senior position where they can show their initiative.
(b) Undertake an education programme to get line managers thinking positively about information management. Remember the difference between making people aware, and equipping them to act. It is the second objective which is crucial here.

These are both long-term actions. This is inevitable, because you are trying to achieve a culture change in a notoriously difficult area.

Do you safeguard the information resource of your organization?

The threat of computer disasters, and the deliberate misuse of information systems, were mentioned on page 114. The term 'information resource' embraces the systems, and the data and information held by them. Both need to be safeguarded. There are many specialist books about data security, but here are some questions which as a senior manager you might wish to explore:

(a) You need an assessment of the threat, covering natural disasters, innocent human mistake, and deliberate human misuse of the system. Quite often fire (arson) is the biggest threat.

(b) You need to judge the size of the loss incurred if the threat succeeds.

(c) You need to judge the extent of the countermeasures which you can reasonably afford. A wide range of physical and electronic measures is available.

(d) You need a security policy which balances the countermeasures with good administrative procedures. The biggest hazard is from internal people; the most boring and inconvenient administrative countermeasures are often the most effective in deterring them.

There are specialist consultancies which can assist in making a security review and developing an appropriate policy.

Do you use the information resource ethically?

Pages 115–118 discussed the wider place of IT in society. As a senior manager, you have a responsibility to the wide range of stakeholders listed. You need to decide whether there is an ethical dimension to this, or whether your policy is merely to comply with the written requirements of the law. It is analogous to deciding your policy about the use of money to 'facilitate' business contracts. You could handle personal data (about living, identifiable individuals) in a way which was contrary to their interests. You could acquire, process and disseminate information about competitors in ways which are contrary to their interests. You must decide whether this is an ethical way to conduct your business, and in your own best long-term interests. As the volume of information held in systems increases, these questions can only become more pressing.

Implementing the action plan

You should now have worked through the hints which relate to the questions at which you scored low during your information management audit. You should thereby have prepared a set of forms from Appendix 2, showing the major impelling and impeding forces, and the personal and team actions you need to take in the short and long term. Having thought it through for yourself, you should 'own' the results, and have confidence that you can achieve results. At this point it would be easy for me to say 'over to you', but a few further tips may be useful:

- Try to get an ally. If you feel you are a lone voice of enlightened information management, try to enlist some support. You know enough about organizational politics and tactics to realize the danger of appearing too evangelical.

- Integrate this action plan alongside the other actions which you progress in your personal time-management system. Make sure you distinguish the urgent from the important; do not neglect longer-term actions because of the pressing nature of shorter-term problems.
- Try to set an example of good information management within your own sphere of responsibility. Your words will then carry greater weight with others.

9   Conclusion

Where are we now?

The aim of this book has been to provide you, as a senior manager, with a framework for assessing and improving the practice of information management in your organization.

The six guidelines which have formed the core of the book are essentially practical, and based upon the current concerns of other senior managers:

1   Establish an information management partnership.
2   Distinguish the potential benefits of IT/IS.
3   Think strategically about information management.
4   Identify the benefits, and their value.
5   Manage the achievement of the benefits.
6   Prepare for the future.

Now that you have considered each of these guidelines in turn, I hope that several points have become clear about how information management needs to be handled in today's organizations:

(a)   You need to demystify the subject, so that it is treated in a manner comparable with other aspects of management.
(b)   You should then deal with it as just one of the items on the agenda of senior managers, attracting an appropriate level of attention throughout your management thinking.
(c)   Like other aspects of management, it requires an effective partnership between all levels of the organization, using a consistent approach.
(d)   You need to 'diverge' and then 'converge' your collective consideration of the subject, if you are to get full value from the developing potential of IT/IS. Too narrow a view will deny you opportunities.
(e)   You need continually to repeat that thinking process, to keep abreast (and

if possible ahead) of the game. This is particularly important if you are trying to sustain competitive advantage with IT/IS. The structure of the book has followed one such cycle, and started you on a second.

As you worked through the book you built up the six-part information management audit. It was suggested in Chapter 8 that you might now wish to repeat that audit in more detail with the help of your colleagues. Eventually, when you are satisfied with the audit, it will answer the question 'Where are we now?' for your enterprise.

Where do we want to be?

The questions of the information management audit provided, in effect, a 'vision' of how this aspect of management should be handled. By your scoring of the questions you identified where you, or your organization, fall short of that vision. Thus you identified what improvements you wish to achieve. This implicitly answers the question 'Where do we want to be?'

How will we get there?

In Chapter 8 you also analysed the problem areas and identified the actions you need to take to solve them. The action plan which you constructed is therefore your 'strategy' for improving your practice of information management. This implicitly answers the question 'How will we get there?'

Congratulations! You have evidently followed the essential steps of strategic thinking (Figure 4.5) in your approach to this aspect of your job. Moreover you should feel equipped to make it happen. If so, this book will have achieved its aim.

If it all seems rather daunting, remember the old adage: 'Be not afraid of moving slowly. Be afraid only of standing still'.

I hope you have enjoyed using the book, and wish you well in implementing your action plan for the benefit of your business!

Appendix 1　Information management audit: forms

The attached forms deal with the six parts of the information management audit. They are similar to the forms presented at the end of Chapters 2–7 inclusive.

Each form relates to one of the guidelines for information management. There are ten questions, based upon the material discussed in the corresponding chapter of the book.

If you copy the forms for management use, remember that they are protected by copyright.

IM Audit - Part 1

Guideline: Establish an information management partnership			
Ser.	Question	Score	Action
1	Is there effective communication between all members of the IM triangle?		
2	Are top managers reluctant to take up IT/IS?		
3	Do top managers relate IT/IS to their business thinking?		
4	Do middle managers/users assess information in product and process?		
5	Do middle managers/users get a sympathetic response to their needs?		
6	Do the senior IT professionals understand the business?		
7	Do the IT professionals work closely with users, to apply IT well?		
8	Do you have a generic policy for IT/IS, related to the business?		
9	Do you have the necessary formal arrangements to control IT/IS?		
10	Are you growing hybrids in the organization?		
	TOTALS		

IM Audit - Part 2

Guideline: Distinguish the potential benefits of IT/IS			
Ser.	Question	Score	Action
1	Do you carefully consider all three generic benefits of IT/IS?		
2	Do you have some systems which seek mainly efficiency benefits?		
3	Can you identify those benefits, and the cost savings?		
4	Do you have some systems which seek mainly effectiveness benefits?		
5	Can you identify those benefits, and the increased return on assets?		
6	Do you have some systems which seek mainly strategic advantage (edge)?		
7	Can you identify those benefits, and the resulting business growth?		
8	Can you provide the right management framework for different benefits?		
9	Can you cope with differences between planned and actual benefits?		
10	Do you have an integrated portfolio for IT/IS?		
	TOTALS		

IM Audit - Part 3

Guideline: Think strategically about information management			
Ser.	Question	Score	Action
1	Do you have senior managers using strategic cognitive skills?		
2	Do you use the three-step creative approach to vision and strategy?		
3	Do you recognize the information aspect of the challenge to managers?		
4	Have you considered the internal view of strategy enough?		
5	Have you considered the external view of strategy enough?		
6	Have you considered the dynamic view of strategy enough?		
7	Can you use the benefit-level matrix to plot the evolution of your IT/IS?		
8	Can you use the BLM to plan ahead, for the industry and your enterprise?		
9	Do you have an information strategy closely linked to business strategy?		
10	Does the information strategy cover business, functionality, and IT/IS?		
	TOTALS		

IM Audit - Part 4

Ser.	Question	Score	Action
Guideline: Identify the benefits, and their value			
1	Is the information strategy a peg in the ground for IS planning?		
2	Does senior management oversee the convergence process of planning?		
3	Do you justify various types of IS according to a consistent set of rules?		
4	Do you recognize, and deal with, the 'must-do' category of IS?		
5	Do you recognize a range of types of business case for IS?		
6	Are numbers used unrealistically, in trying to quantify benefits?		
7	Could you sharpen up the way you make the business case?		
8	Is your investment culture the same for IS as for other resources?		
9	Do you package proposals, in order to match the investment culture?		
10	Do you consciously balance risk and return, for IS investment?		
	TOTALS		

IM Audit - Part 5

Ser.	Question	Score	Action
Guideline: Manage the achievement of the benefits			
1	Do you manage information systems as people, procedures and technology?		
2	Do you give the right balance of management attention to these three?		
3	Do you know the project life-cycle, or equivalent, used in your business?		
4	Do you consciously adapt it for urgent or complex cases?		
5	Do you know what threats your people perceive from IT/IS?		
6	Do you take appropriate action, at the right time in the project life-cycle?		
7	Do you consciously practise benefit management for IT/IS?		
8	Are requirements and benefits defined and agreed together, by users?		
9	Is the achievement of the benefits monitored, in subsequent operation?		
10	Does senior management monitor progress, or have witch-hunts afterwards?		
	TOTALS		

IM Audit – Part 6

Ser.	Question	Score	Action
	Guideline: Prepare for the future		
1	Do you review your information strategy regularly?		
2	Are you always ready for a diverge-converge discussion about IT/IS?		
3	Have you learnt the historical lessons from the evolution of your IT/IS?		
4	Do you keep abreast of IT developments and opportunities?		
5	Do you have an effective combination of man and machine?		
6	Are you consciously building the new organization?		
7	Are you using IT/IS fully to support that?		
8	Do you have infopreneurs in your organization?		
9	Do you safeguard the information resource of your organization?		
10	Do you use the information resource ethically?		
	TOTALS		

Appendix 2   Action-plan forms

The attached blank forms are working documents to help you construct an action plan, based upon your information management audit. The procedure is detailed in Chapter 8.

If you copy the forms for management use, remember that they are protected by copyright.

Action-Plan Form

Ser	Problem	Forces		Personal actions		Team actions		Remarks
		Impelling	Impeding	Short-term	Long-term	Short-term	Long-term	

Action–Plan Form

Ser	Problem	Forces Impelling | Impeding	Personal actions Short- term | Long- term	Team actions Short- term | Long- term	Remarks

Index